FLO

By the staff of Berlitz Guides

7th Printing
1986/1987 Edition

How to use our guide

- All the practical information, hints and tips that you will need before and during the trip start on page 103, with a complete rundown of contents on page 106.
- For general background, see the sections Florida and the Floridians, p. 6, and A Brief History, p. 12.
- All the sights to see are listed between pages 23 and 82. Our own choice of sights most highly recommended is pin-pointed by the Berlitz traveller symbol.
- Entertainment, nightlife and all other leisure activities are described between pages 83 and 95, while information on restaurants and cuisine is to be found on pages 96 to 102.
- Finally, there is an index at the back of the book, pp. 127–128.

Although we make every effort to ensure the accuracy of all the information in this book, changes occur incessantly. We cannot therefore take responsibility for facts, prices, addresses and circumstances in general that are constantly subject to alteration. Our guides are updated on a regular basis as we reprint, and we are always grateful to readers who let us know of any errors, changes or serious omissions they come across.

Text: George Rumens
Photography: Jacques Bétant
Layout: Doris Haldemann
We are particularly grateful to Harriet Brunner for her help in the preparation of this book. We also wish to thank the News Bureau of the Florida Department of Commerce and the Miami Beach Tourist Development Authority for their valuable assistance.

Cartography: Falk-Verlag, Hamburg.

Contents

Cover picture: Swimming pool, Fontainebleau Hilton.

Florida and the Floridians

Jutting from Georgia nearly to Cuba, this sun-blessed peninsula—bigger than all England—is home for spacemen and sports stars, millionaires and pensioners. Not to mention pink flamingoes, jumping dolphins and Mickey Mouse.

Fast and trendy, Florida matches California as the pacesetter in new American ideas about sports and entertainment and making the most of life among the gifts of nature. The Sunshine State has gone international, attracting the most unlikely combination of immigrants, tourists and seekers after the good life. Moguls from South America, sun-starved British holidaymakers, newcomers from Caribbean islands and refugees from the New York rat-race all agree on the virtues of palmshaded life somewhere

between the Atlantic and the Gulf. They're even ready to put up with mosquitos, alligators and hurricanes for it.

The most southerly of the continental states (only Hawaii is closer to the equator), Florida endures scorching summers in exchange for mild winters. Floridians and visitors smugly read the headlines about fogs and snows dislocating the cities of the north while Miami basks in the nation's highest temperatures.

Topographically Florida is less exciting: a flat plain with the highest point a mere 345 feet above sea level. The coastline stretches 1,350 miles, longer than any state's save Alaska. All along the offshore islands, pelicans reconnoitre above the waves, exquisitely coloured shells roll in the surf

A perfectly restored "Excalibur" on Daytona Beach, a bright smile at Disney World: everything's better in the Florida sunshine.

The Ethnic Mix

Florida's kinship to the rest of America's Deep South can be felt mostly in the north of the state, around Tallahassee and Jacksonville, strongly Anglo-Saxon in origin. But from the beginning of its Spanish discovery, the state has always had a pronounced Latin flavour. The steady flow of Cubans into Miami, the Keys and all along the South Florida coast lends great colour to the street life and a tingling spice to the cuisine. The Cubans, even second generation, are fiercely loyal to a certain image of the "old country" and always vociferous about the political ferment that bubbles just 90 miles from Key West. The Caribbean influence is reinforced by the increasing immigration of Haitians.

But Florida is above all a magnet for New Yorkers, fleeing the cold winters and smoggy summers of the Big Apple. The accents in the supermarkets and around the swimming pools are more likely to be laced with the heavy ironies of Brooklyn and Queens than the back-slapping good-ole-boy cheerfulness of the nearer neighbour states of Georgia or South Carolina. Then the Keys themselves have attracted a cosmopolitan mixture of bohemians—artists, writers and plain old beach-bums—from all over America and beyond, a lively bunch of eccentrics who defy any ethnic classification at all. Key West does have one proud ethnic minority: the "Conchs" (named after the conch shellfish). They trace their ancestry back to the American Revolution when loyalists to the British crown fled first to the Bahamas and then on to the Keys, where their community still thrives in the fishing business and keeps aloof from other "interlopers".

and an occasional giant turtle might be seen wading ashore. Inland, grassy plains shimmering with an estimated 30,000 lakes are divided into cattle ranches, fragrant orange groves, pine and cypress forests and homely small towns. Adding to the colour, flaming bougainvillea covers the clapboard houses of Key West, and exotic flowers abound.

From the inland lakes, the overflow of warm water seeps through hundreds of square miles of grassland culminating in the mangrove swamps of

8

Florida is half water, with thousands of lakes and miles of canals. Sunny days also make it a haven for retirement (see previous page).

the Everglades, pride of southern Florida. Here you can sail, fish or explore the trails in search of alligators, southern bald eagles or the elusive Florida panther.

For swimmers and seaside fans, there are miles of palm-fringed beaches. The ocean is warm, thanks to the Gulf Stream; refreshments are almost always nearby and it is easy to make friends with other vacationers or plan tomorrow's excursion to one of Florida's famous attractions.

Up and down the state, you'll come across sights normally seen only on television. Whether it's a giant Saturn rocket, an Indian wrestling with an alligator, or the world's

largest collection of sea shells, you'll be overwhelmed by dozens of fascinating things to see and do.

Apart from Disney World—the world's most popular tourist attraction—the seas round Florida have given rise to a show of another kind. In the aquarium spectaculars you'll see schools of trained dolphins displaying their splashy skills, killer whales leaping out of the water, sharks devouring their lunchtime snacks in an ecstasy of wild thrashing and other exotic ocean curiosities.

But, most of all, a holiday in Florida will be an opportunity to try your hand at any one of a number of outdoor sports. Water-skiing, fishing, scuba-diving, sailing, surfing or canoeing, tennis, golf and riding—whatever you try, a friendly instructor will be close at hand to give advice. Many resorts feature video-equipped tennis and golf "clinics", where you can improve your game.

Dining in Florida is informal and indulged in with great gusto. Portions are gargantuan; eating and drinking goes on at all times of the day and night. Choose stone crabs (a Florida delicacy) or a live lobster from a tank; go out to a traditional barbecue, or venture into one of Miami's Cuban restaurants for something really special.

Florida's appeal is irresistible. Thousands of new settlers arrive weekly, abandon their overcoats and put on leisure suits—or change to cut-off shorts, sports shirts and sandals. And if, under a velvet Miami night sky with a *piña colada* in your hand, you say that you'd like to stay, Floridians will laugh and say they know the feeling. It is called "getting sand in your shoes". **11**

A Brief History

Long before vacationers ever thought of sunning themselves on Miami Beach, prehistoric animals enjoyed Florida's balmy climate. Sabre-toothed tigers prowled through the swamps. Woolly mammoths, giant bison and even camels roamed the plains—not surprising when you consider that the state is on the same latitude as the Sahara desert.

Men first wandered into Florida about 15,000 years ago. They survived by hunting and fishing until around 1000 B.C., when someone discovered that despite the land's low-fertility soil, the generous climate made it possible to cultivate crops, including maize, squash, cassava, and peppers. By the standards of prehistoric times, these early Floridians were well off. Plentiful game and fish, bountiful harvests, native tools and pots, even artwork such as statuettes and shell jewellery enriched their lives. On the eve of the European discovery of the New World, Florida's indigenous population numbered some 25,000 souls, divided into five nations. Chief of these were the Timuca and Apalachee.

Florida—Facts and Figures

Much of the information given below will be found elsewhere in our guide; it has been gathered together here for a quick briefing.

Population: 8,500,000

Geography: 58,560 sq. miles in area with the second-longest coastline (1,350 miles) in the U.S.

Capital: Tallahassee (population 85,000).

Climate: Semi-tropical in the southern half of the state, less extreme in northern areas; sunshine can be relied upon most of the year; humidity may be very high in summer. The hurricane season runs from June to November. Early-warning systems permit precautions to be taken.

Economy: Tourism, citrus fruit and vegetable growing, tobacco, food processing, chemicals, electrical and transportation equipment.

Get there: Jet flight from New York 2½ hours, London 10 hours.

European Discovery

Christopher Columbus was not far from Florida when he bumped into the island of Hispaniola (Haiti and Dominican Republic) on his way to "the Indies" in 1492. While other early explorers may have wandered up and down the Florida coast searching for the elusive passage to the Pacific, credit for the discovery of the land goes to Juan Ponce de León (1460–1521), a Spanish nobleman. Bored with life in Spain after the Moorish wars were ended, Ponce de León set out with Columbus on the second expedition to Hispaniola in 1493. The excitement of the voyage rekindled his taste for adventure and by 1508, Ponce was on his way to Puerto Rico as his own master. He became the island's governor, but soon lost his position to the more influential Diego Columbus, son of the great navigator.

In 1512, the Spanish king commissioned Ponce de León to discover and explore the fabled "Isle of Bimini". The island, so the legend said, concealed a spring with the miraculous power to restore youth to the aged. No doubt Ponce, who was 52 years old at the time, was attracted by the lure of instant youth. But should he fail to find the precious fountain, he could depend—or so he thought—on gold, trade with the natives, and slave labour to provide for a comfortable old age.

Setting sail for the Bahamas in search of Bimini, Ponce landed instead on the Florida coast, on April 2nd, 1513. He named the new country after the date in his calendar, *Pascua Florida*, the Feast of Flowers at Easter. From his first landfall, near present-day St. Augustine, Ponce and his trusty crew sailed down the coast, past Cape Canaveral, along the Florida Keys and out to the Dry Tortugas. From there, they continued north along the Gulf coast to Charlotte Harbor—perhaps beyond—before returning to Puerto Rico after the eight-month voyage. In his sea-rovings, Ponce had missed Bimini, but he had discovered instead an immense land full of promise. His grateful sovereign granted him the right to conquer, govern and colonize the territory.

Early Colonies

Ponce's discovery was later to prove a bitter disappointment. Setting out hopefully on his second voyage to Florida in 1521, the explorer took along two ships, 200 colonists, live- **13** stock and farm implements. Though Ponce knew the Indians at Charlotte Harbor were hostile, he chose to land there nevertheless. But as his party were building shelters, fierce warriors attacked. Ponce himself was badly wounded by an arrow, and was carried back to his flagship. By the time the disillusioned settlers reached Cuba, their leader was near death. He was buried in Puerto Rico.

The pattern of great expectations and dashed hopes was to repeat itself in later colonial ventures. Pánfilo de Narváez, a follower of Cortés, set out from Cuba in 1528 with 600 soldiers and colonists, but lost a full 200 of his party before even reaching Tampa Bay. Marching inland, they expected to find food and water easily, but they almost starved. The fabled gold of the Indians was nowhere to be found, the only inhabitants being poor Indian women and children living in mud huts. Panic-stricken by their plight in a strange and hostile land, Narváez and his followers quickly built makeshift boats and set

Pedro Menéndez de Avilés founded St. Augustine (1565). Daunting stone bulwarks kept pirates away.

sail for Mexico, which they thought was nearby. The voyage, doomed from the outset, was a disaster. Of the 242 men who manned the boats, only four ever reached Mexico City. Narváez was not among the survivors. A search party sent out by Narváez's wife also disappeared.

Yet another ill-famed expedition to Florida was led by Hernando de Soto. Already rich and famous at the age of 36, the Spanish explorer left Cuba on an expedition to Florida in 1538. An army of 600 enthusiastic volunteers set sail with him. When they landed in Tampa Bay on May 30, 1539, they were met by Juan Ortiz, a survivor from the search party sent out to find Narváez. Ortiz could now speak the Indian languages, and was to prove invaluable as a guide and interpreter. But this auspicious beginning was not followed by similar good fortune. Though de Soto's band marched incredible distances—as far as Oklahoma and Kansas—in search of fabulous riches, they found none. The further they went, the more determined they became to continue until they discovered something, but they never did. Half of the men—including de Soto him-

self—died during the four-years' march. The disappointed survivors made their way back to Cuba empty-handed.

The First Permanent Settlement

In 1565 Spain succeeded in founding a colony that was to last for centuries. On September 8th of that year, Pedro Menéndez de Avilés and a detachment of soldiers arrived at the mouth of the St. John's river near present-day Jacksonville. Here they came upon a party of French Huguenots who had been struggling along for a year in their small settlement of Fort Caroline.

At this time the two great European nations were engaged in bitter warfare for colonial domination, and a battle was certain. The Spaniards caught the French completely by surprise, and easily overcame Fort Caroline. Faced with the problem of what to do with so many captives, Menéndez decided that the threat to his own small party with its limited food supply was too great to ignore. Sparing women and children, Catholics, fifers, drummers and trumpeters, he put the rest of the Frenchmen to the sword "not as Frenchmen, but as Lutherans".

Menéndez then travelled about 30 miles south and founded the first permanent settlement in North America, the colony of St. Augustine. It suffered from sporadic Indian attacks and in the year 1586 was raided by the swashbuckling English privateer Sir Francis Drake. The difficulties of defending the Florida outpost were becoming plain, but its strategic importance was judged essential, and in response to later English assaults the Spanish constructed a massive fortress of stone.

Battle for Power

The English were not the only ambitious nation to worry the Spanish lords of Florida. In 1682, Robert Cavelier Sieur de La Salle completed his long journey down the Mississippi, claiming the entire river valley for the king of France. With the English to the north and the French to the west, Spanish possessions in America were seriously threatened.

Bold moves by Louis XIV of France upset the diplomatic balance in the New World as well as the Old. When Louis attempted to seat his grandson on the throne of Spain, England was quick to see the threat. Spain and France united could dictate to the rest of Europe and the world. The War of the Spanish Succession in 1702 brought English forces deep into Florida. Though the mighty fortress at St. Augustine presented a problem, the rest of Florida's meagre defences did not, and in the four subsequent years of fighting, the English wiped out most of Spain's military outposts and religious missions.

With Spain less of a threat, the English and French could concentrate on winning total domination of colonial North America. The Seven Years' War in Europe spread to the New World as the French and Indian War. Despite Indian support, the French forces went down to defeat from Quebec to Florida, leaving the British as virtual masters of the continent. In 1763, Florida was officially ceded to England.

When the English took over, the Spaniards moved out to a man. Along with the change in European overlords came another population change. Descendants of the original Timuca and Apalachee Indians, decimated by European diseases, the slave trade and internal feuds, left Florida along with the Spaniards to find more peaceful homes in the West and in Cuba. As they departed, their farms and villages were taken over by Seminoles from neighbouring Alabama and Georgia.

The Seminoles were eagerly courted by English traders bearing pots, blankets, knives, guns and axes. Trade was profitable; the English had found a way of making gold where the Spanish had failed to find it. The British colonial government encouraged settlement, farming and mining. Large grants were freely made to enterprising settlers to organize plantations. Soon indigo, rice, turpentine, sugar and oranges became valuable cargoes for the colonial trade.

A Lost Colony, A New State
In a bizarre twist of international diplomacy, Florida reverted to Spanish rule under the terms of the Treaty of Paris of 1783. But the allegiance of Florida's Seminole and European inhabitants remained with Great Britain, which had done so much to develop the land. After several decades of unhappy Spanish rule, West Florida petitioned to join the newly independent United States of America. Annexation came in the early 1800s, but the East remained a battleground where Spanish, British, Seminoles and Americans fought to control the future of **17**

the region. Among others to join the fray in Florida was the colourful future U.S. president, Andrew Jackson. In the early 19th century, the battle was over, and Spain, nominal ruler of Florida, ceded control to the United States. By 1845, Florida was a full-fledged state, the 27th in the Union.

With annexation, American settlers flooded into Florida, causing consternation among the long-time inhabitants. The Seminoles were the most affected, and though some chiefs accepted a government offer to move to new lands in the frontier territories to the west, others stood and fought. The Seminole War of 1835–42 brought a violent conclusion to the conflict. After the war only a few hundred Seminoles remained in small, widely scattered villages.

Florida took the side of the southern states in the American Civil War, first proclaiming its independence from the Union, and then joining the Confederate States. But in a replay of the Spanish-English conflict, Union forces from the north easily captured and occupied Florida's strategic points.

Above: Henry Flagler's mansion. Below: Florida "citrus gold".

The Tourist Boom

As the Union soldiers manned their posts in Florida's settlements and ports, they noticed something that a small number of sun-seekers had discovered even before the Civil War: the winter months came, but the cold weather didn't. However it wasn't until the last quarter of the 19th century, that a number of enterprising businessmen suddenly saw the real potential of the state's geography and climate. Of them, two names stand out: Henry Morrison Flagler and Henry Bradley Plant. Both men possessed the kind of pioneering and imaginative spirit that was the driving force of the late 19th century. In addition, they had the ability to realize their dreams. Flagler's East Coast Railroad drove its tracks right through swamp, jungle and even over the ocean to Key West; and Henry Plant's development of the Atlantic Coast system opened up central and western Florida.

Now that you could get there, tourists began to arrive. Before long the word was out: Florida was a fabulous place to spend the winter. Between 1870 and 1890, Florida's population doubled, and it has continued to grow ever since. **19**

The tourist boom became a near riot in the mid 1920s when real estate prices began to soar. Suddenly, thousands of Americans wanted to own a piece of Florida for vacations, retirement, or just as a speculative investment. Prices climbed to astronomical heights. Over 2,000 arrivals a day flooded into the state, and soon the railroads forbade any car to

Miami Beach real estate is some of America's most expensive. Where do you build when there's none left? Straight up (Fontainebleau Hilton).

advertise Miami as its destination. Then, reality began to redress the balance. A ship from up north carrying would-be Floridians sank in Biscayne Bay; a hurricane in 1926 wreaked havoc in the city; the bottom fell out of land prices, and the boom was over.

Florida's economy didn't

Hurricane Who?

Alice, Betty or Carol? Or Arthur, Bobby or Cyril? Thus the controversy has raged between women's liberation movements and traditionalists at the meteorological office over the naming of hurricanes. But, whatever people call them doesn't make much difference to these frighteningly powerful tropical storms which sweep through Florida from time to time with winds of up to 150 miles an hour.

The raging gales, shrieking winds and flood tides may sound exciting to an outsider but, in fact, they're terrifying and often tragic.

The most famous hurricane in living memory was in 1926. During a lull in that storm, when the "eye" (the calm centre of the hurricane) passed over Miami, thousands of relieved people went out, thinking it was finished, only to be caught up in the second half a while later. Over 100 people were killed and hundreds of millions of dollars of damage was caused.

Today, meterologists spend hours trying to work out when the next storm will arrive, but even weathermen and their sophisticated computers are helpless when confronted by the awesome fury and unpredictable track of a hurricane.

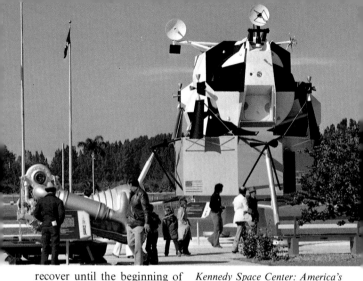

Kennedy Space Center: America's moon lander back on Florida soil.

recover until the beginning of World War II when thousands of new recruits arrived to be trained and equipped at the state's military bases. These modern soldiers fell under the same spell as others had before them. When peace came, remembering the warmth of the southern sun, many returned to Florida to start businesses, raise families, and later, to retire. The state's economy was diversified. Agriculture was expanded to provide winter vegetables and fruit for the export market, especially citrus. Beef and dairy farms profited from cheap land prices in Florida's interior. Entrepreneurs found it easy to set up shop in a place where people were glad to live. The 1959 revolution in Cuba brought many families in search of a new life, swelling Miami's population and adding to growth.

Despite ups and downs caused by fashionable fads, recent decades have seen no let-up in the general Florida boom. Jumbo jets bring enthusiastic vacationers in greater numbers than ever before. Sun-seekers happily buzz down from frigid northern cities in just a few pleasant hours. And European travellers, off on a warm-winter American adventure, find Miami one of the New World's most accessible cities by air.

But "air travel" has yet another dimension in Florida, for it was from Cape Canaveral on the state's Atlantic coast that America's first rockets probed outer space. Beginning in 1950 with the launch of a modified German V-2 rocket, Cape Canaveral saw the blast-off of innumerable vehicles, each more sophisticated and powerful than the last. From the Cape's Kennedy Space Center, American astronauts were lifted majestically on man's first flight to the moon in 1969.

The *conquistadores* searched the length and breadth of Florida looking for the elusive fountain of youth and fabled treasure. Four centuries later, Floridians and visitors are finding rejuvenation on sunny beaches, and incredible wealth in the richness of the land. But the period of discovery is not over, for even today you'll sense the booming frontier atmosphere of a state progressing towards a dynamic future. And one that looks even brighter in the sunshine.

Where to Go

In terms of size, Florida ranks only 22nd among American states; but, in its more than 58,000 square miles of territory (the size of England and Wales combined), there's enough to see and do for several months —let alone the average two-week holiday.

In this book we travel north from Miami through the Gold Coast resorts of Fort Lauderdale, Boca Raton and Palm Beach to St. Augustine. Then we look at Disney World and Central Florida before going south to the Everglades and Key West, and north-west, up the Gulf Coast. But preceding any of these comes the dowager duchess of American vacation spots...

Miami Beach

The city of Miami Beach, the place "where the sun spends the winter", is in fact a narrow 7-mile strip of land separated from mainland Miami by Biscayne Bay and connected to it by causeways. It's here that you'll find the opulent hotels and extravagant tastes that have become just as much a part of the American legend as the Wild West.

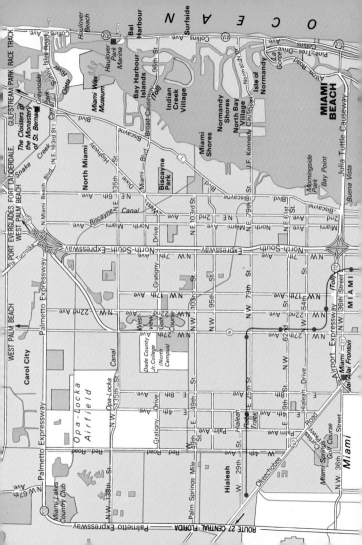

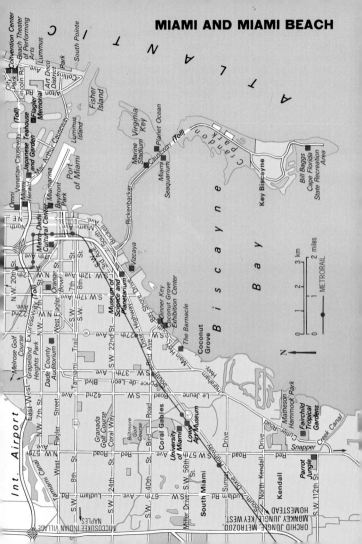

MIAMI AND MIAMI BEACH

ATLANTIC

City Park Convention Center
Beach Theater of Performing Arts
Lincoln Rd.
South Pointe Park
Lummus
Collins Ave.
Art Deco District
Flagler Memorial (Toll)
Japanese Teahouse and Garden
Alton Rd.
Fisher Island
Venetian Causeway
Miami Herald
Mar Arthur Causeway
Lummus Island
Omni
Japanese Teahouse
Port of Miami
Miamarina
Bayfront Park
N.E.
Mar Arthur Causeway

Virginia Key
Marine Stadium
Miami Seaquarium
Planet Ocean
Crandon Park
Bill Baggs Cape Florida State Recreation Area
Key Biscayne

North
Metro-Dade Cultural Center
Rickenbacker Causeway (Toll)

B i s c a y n e   B a y

N.W. 20th St.
12th Ave.
22nd Ave.
Grapeland Expressway (Toll)
Heights Park
Melrose Golf Course
East-West N.W. 7th St.
West Flagler St.
Orange Bowl
Dade County Auditorium
N.W. 7th Ave.
S.W. 8th St.
S.W. 7th St.
3rd Ave.
Museum of Science and Planetarium
Vizcaya
Dinner Key
Coconut Grove Exhibition Center
The Barnacle
Coconut Grove

3 km
2 miles
METRORAIL
2
1
1
0
0

N

Int. Airport

Tamiami Canal Rd.
N.W. 7th St.
Granada Golf Course
West Flagler St.
42nd Ave.
Tamiami Trail
Le Jeune Road
Ponce-de-Leon Blvd.
S.W. 37th Ave.
S.W. 27th Ave.
S.W. 22nd Ave.
17th Ave.
Dixie Highway
South Dixie Highway
Bird Ave.
Main Hwy.
Tigertail Ave.
Hatahan Hwy.

Coral Gables
University of Miami
Lowe Art Museum
Biltmore Golf Course
Coral Gables
S.W. 57th Ave.
S.W. 56th Ave.
Bird Road
Red Road
Granada Golf Course
Ludlam Rd.
S.W. 24th St.
S.W. 40th St.
Miller Drive
Bird Drive
S.W. 8th St.
South Miami
Sunset Drive
South Dixie Highway
Kendall Drive
North Kendall Drive
Cutler Road
Snapper Creek Canal
Matheson Hammock Park
Fairchild Tropical Gardens

Red Road
South Dixie Highway
Kendall
Parrot Jungle
S.W. 112th St.

NAPLES
MICCOSUKEE INDIAN VILLAGE
ORCHID JUNGLE METROZOO
MONKEY JUNGLE KEY WEST
HOMESTEAD

For the visitor to Miami Beach, a drive along **Collins Avenue** is an education in itself. Lining this street are the vast pleasure palaces whose rooms, comfortable coffee shops, bars and swimming pools are packed full in the high season.

The heyday of the lavish resort reached its peak in the 1950s, but even now the proliferation of hotels—built one after another, cheek by jowl—will astound you. Today these establishments try to outdo each other in offering special rates, but it's not difficult to imagine how just a few decades ago competition between

them was based on which was the largest, richest and most luxurious.

In stark contrast are the more modest art deco hotels of South Beach, a somewhat run-down area developed between the world wars and now undergoing revitalization. Thanks to the extraordinary number of buildings in the streamlined style, one square mile, known as the **art deco district,** has been declared a

Electric island? Million-dollar mile? Much of Miami's excitement comes from its rich ethnic mix. The beach is big enough for all.

national preservation zone. Nowhere else in America is there such a concentration of architecture from the 1930s and '40s. The Miami Design Preservation League organizes guided tours of this unique quarter (tel. 672-2014).

The Miami Beach business district, just north of South Beach, contains Lincoln Road Mall, a pedestrian shopping street. Most of the inexpensive and modestly priced accommodations lie between South Beach and 41st Street; then, above Arthur Godfrey Boulevard, are the top-of-the-line hotels, including the legendary **Fontainebleau Hilton.** The "Fountain-Blow", as it is pronounced, is a resort in itself, with pools, cabanas, waterfalls, cave-grottoes, hidden bars, shops, a drugstore, a tennis centre and an aquarium. Behind the recently modernized and redecorated rooms of the hotel lingers the nostalgia of an America now only available on film. Jayne Mansfield, Frank Sinatra, Dean Martin and other Hollywood stars stayed at the Fontainebleau.

The rambling Miami Beach **boardwalk** begins at 21st Street and runs out along the water, behind the big hotels, as far as 46th. The wooden walkway made an immediate

hit when it opened in 1984. Covered pavilions provide a place to sit and contemplate the panorama of sea and sky.

Continuing north the A1A road winds through the pleasant resort of SURFSIDE, smart BAL HARBOUR with its waffle-faced condominiums and elegant hotels. Don't miss **Bal Harbour Shops,** a luxury mall renowned as much for its setting as the merchandise on sale. You'll find some of America's best department stores here, as well as many fine boutiques and restaurants. (Worth a detour!) Further along A1A you come to Haulover Park, sandwiched between the bay and the ocean. On the bay side, Haulover Marina has berths for dozens of sportfishing boats. The ocean side of the park has an acceptable family beach, with picnic places.

The sand, sea, sun and hotels of Miami Beach may well leave you feeling that for once the description "fabulous" might not be an exaggeration. But, as evening approaches, many pile into their cars and stream back over the strip's five causeways to the excitements of the mainland.

Older folks seek shelter from it, but the younger ones never seem to get enough of it: sun.

Miami

This baffling, infuriating hodgepodge of a town boasts dozens of different styles of architecture, a wide variety of activities and entertainments and dozens of tourist attractions as well.

The Metrorail elevated railway brings people from the northern and southern suburbs into the city centre, while the automated Metromover provides rapid transit within the downtown district. Be sure to go for a ride!

Revival is definitely in the air on **Flagler Street,** the heart of downtown Miami. Dade County's most prestigious cultural complex, the **Metro-Dade Cultural Center,** opened at 101 West Flagler in 1983. The arcaded, Mediterranean-style building was designed in the post-Modernist style by the eminent architectural firm of Johnson and Burgee. Under one roof are the **Center for the Fine Arts** (an art gallery and sculpture court provide space for a series of temporary exhibitions), an auditorium, Miami's central public library and the **South Florida Historical Museum.** This last features dozens of fascinating "hands-on" displays. You can, for example, set the sails and haul the rigging on an old sailing boat—symbol of Florida's pioneer era.

The other principal downtown thoroughfare, **Biscayne Boulevard,** doubles as the site of Miami's Grand Prix and the famed annual Orange Bowl Parade on New Year's Eve. Occupying a sizeable portion of prime Boulevard real estate is the **Omni** centre, a huge shopping, entertainment and hotel complex with movie theatres and restaurants.

Bayfront Park extends from Biscayne Boulevard to Biscayne Bay. A waterfront promenade is under construction, along with the Bayside shopping complex. The new facility incorporates **Miamarina,** a pier with yacht berths and restaurants. Across a drawbridge is the enormous ocean-going Port of Miami, from which liners and cruise-ships depart for the West Indies, Mexico and South America.

Go back to Biscayne Boulevard and continue along it to the marble skyscraper Pavillon hotel and office complex, a striking Miami landmark. At this point, the Boulevard runs into Du Pont Plaza, an up-and-coming centre of international banking and business with a concentration of ultra-modern luxury hotels. Fronting on the plaza are the **Miami Convention Center** (400 S.E. 2nd Ave.), a 5,000-seat venue for concerts and special events, and the University of Miami Conference Center, which can accommodate up to 500. They adjoin the Hyatt Regency Miami hotel overlooking Miami River.

Cross the river and head along **Brickell Avenue.** Here you'll be able to admire some of Miami's finest high-rise office buildings, banks and elegant apartment complexes.

While **Little Havana** has its beginnings in downtown Miami, the centre of the district is a 30-block-long section further west along 8th Street, called "Calle Ocho". Restaurants

Coconut Grove footpaths are just right for freewheeling rollerskaters.

here specialize in Cuban and Spanish-style cuisine and street-side snack bars serve up strong and aromatic *café cubano*. Lots of small businesses flourish in the area, too. It's estimated that over 500,000 Cubans now live in Miami—making them the largest ethnic group of the city's two million population. But it's along "Calle Ocho" that traditions linger most palpably.

To the south-west lies the wealthy community of CORAL GABLES, full of fountains, tropical gardens and Spanish architecture, and **Coconut Grove,** a youthful residential area on the shores of the bay. The "Grove", with its cosy little shops, bikeways, roller-skating girls in the parks, live theatre and sheltered harbour packed with pelicans and bobbing sailboats, is one of the liveliest places in town.

The large number of tourist attractions in the greater Miami area are all widely scattered. Don't forget that the scale of the grid-shaped street maps often make distances look deceptive. A car ride from say Coral Gables to downtown Miami would take from 25 to 30 minutes. Below are some of the sights (grouped according to special interest) you won't want to miss in Miami.

Animals, Tropical Plants, Marine Life

Average temperatures in southern Florida range between 70 °F in winter and 81 °F in summer. An ideal climate, naturalists will tell you, for the proliferation of tropical flora and fauna in all its manifold forms.

Pride of the city is one of the world's largest tropical aquariums, the Miami **Sea-quarium,** off the Rickenbacker Causeway. (It's a 20-minute bus ride from downtown along the causeway to the entrance gates.) The complex is situated in a park circled by a mono-rail. The variety of water-shows are timed so that specta-tors can move from one to an-other to see everything. Shows (which vary) may include the feeding of a canal full of sharks; a troop of performing sea-lions; the antics of Flipper, the famous dolphin who once had his own TV show, and a show in which a huge killer

whale leaps out of its pool and drenches the audience.

The Seaquarium is one of the few places in the world where the rare manatee or sea-cow can be seen. This large seal-like creature used to live in vast numbers in Florida's waterways before the advent of propeller-driven speed boats, which killed many of them. Now they're in danger of extinction.

Across the highway from Seaquarium, **Planet Ocean** presents exhibits and films with a more scientific approach to oceanography and ecology. You could spend hours in the fascinating centre, which contains a full-sized submarine among other exhibits.

Go back to the main road and continue along it another half-mile to the centre of KEY BISCAYNE. The northern part of the island is given over to **Crandon Park,** a vast public beach with picnic facilities. Don't pick the sea oats that line this and other Florida beaches; they prevent erosion of the sand. South again lies **Bill Baggs Cape Florida State Recreation Area,** site of the historic Cape Florida light-

At Parrot Jungle, you can feed— and even talk to—the animals.

house (built in 1825 and reactivated in 1978). Ask at the entrance gate about guided tours of the Keeper's house (restored to its 1836 appearance) and the lighthouse itself. You won't soon forget the 95-foot climb up into the lantern. Nor the spectacular view. Afterwards, relax on the beach or walk along the nature trails.

South on Old Cutler Road, the **Fairchild Tropical Garden** contains over 80 acres of tropical plants, trees, shrubs and flowers. Near the park, just off 57th Avenue, **Parrot Jungle's** macaws, flamingoes and other exotic birds fly freely through huge aviaries. Parrots will eat out of your hand, trained birds ride bicycles, roller skate, count and fascinate the kids with their tricks.

Wild animals run free at the cageless **Metrozoo**, south again at 12400 S.W. 152nd Street. This is one of the largest and most modern zoos in the U.S., home to white Bengal tigers, Siamese crocodiles, gorillas, giraffes and many species more. Don't miss the petting zoo, elephant rides and shows. The vast aviary shelters hundreds of exotic birds.

Farther out of town, about an hour south of Miami, the **Monkey Jungle** will provide an unusual experience, for the public are caged and the monkeys go free. See the tiny primates swing, dive and climb in the colourful, cultivated tropical jungle. In the same area, one of the world's largest outdoor orchid gardens can be found at the **Orchid Jungle.**

For **Hialeah Park** in northwest Miami, see p. 86.

For **Hialeah Park** in northwest Miami, see p. 86.

Biscayne National Park offers snorkelling, swimming, picnicking and nature walks in and around Elliot Key—a rare tropical hardwood forest preserved in its natural state—and 23 attendant islets. Park boats ferry visitors some 7 miles out to the site from Convoy Point near Homestead. Write or telephone in advance for information and reservations: P.O. Box 1369, Homestead, Florida (tel. 247-PARK).

Museums

If you get caught in a tropical storm, or want a change from the beach, pay a visit to one of Miami's various museums.

The **Center for the Fine Arts** on Flagler Street stages excellent temporary shows. See page 30.

See page 30.

The **Lowe Art Museum** (on the University of Miami campus in Coral Gables) displays a permanent exhibition ranging from Primitive and American 35

Indian art to 20th century works.

The **Vizcaya Museum of Art and Gardens,** on South Bayshore Drive, is one of Florida's unique attractions. The 70-room Italianate palace was built by American millionaire tractor manufacturer James Deering. It's fitted out with valuable antique furniture, textiles and *objets d'art.*

Opposite Vizcaya, the **Museum of Science** features 70 "hands-on" exhibits, while the adjacent **Space Transit Planetarium** screens a fascinating series of changing shows that highlight various aspects of astronomy.

Back on Biscayne Boulevard and even further north you'll come to **St. Bernard's Monastery,** "the oldest building in North America". In actual fact, the 12th-century cloisters were shipped over in blocks by millionaire William Randolph Hearst in 1925 from Segovia, Spain. Antiques and works of art are on display inside.

For an up-to-the-minute briefing on the smaller art galleries, museums and more ephemeral attractions, consult a weekly what's on magazine.

Villa Vizcaya, a sumptuous setting for Dade County Art Museum.

The Gold Coast

There are at least five different roads leading north along this celebrated 70-mile stretch of Atlantic coastline. The older highways US 1 and US 441 lie inland from the coast; I-95 is the free multi-lane Interstate expressway, best used if you want to travel fast; the Florida turnpike is for long distances and A1A is the coastal road, with nice views but it's slow going and there are traffic lights.

The long coast includes half a dozen of Florida's most famous winter resorts. At first glance it's difficult to distinguish between them, but the beach cities all have sufficient individuality to inspire fierce loyalties in the hearts of their regular visitors.

All resorts are characterized by wide boulevards, whitewashed banks, motels, hotels, condominiums and a good selection of restaurants. You can walk for miles on long sandy beaches, while above the waves, graceful seagulls fly in formation along the length of the rollers.

The first rather quiet resort north of Miami is HOLLY-WOOD, with five miles of glorious beach. The Chamber of Commerce here will inform **37**

A cruise on a paddlewheel river-boat is a Fort Lauderdale treat.

you about the annual Seven Lively Arts Festival. DANIA, north-west of Hollywood, is known locally as "the antique capital of Florida". All along US 1 dealers have set up shops in the sunshine. Dania also has its own Jai Alai Fronton.

Lively and sometimes outrageous, **Fort Lauderdale** **38** straddles 165 miles of inland waterway. The endangered manatee (a relative of the elephant) is sometimes seen in quieter rivers, trying to keep out of the way of an estimated 30,000 private boats and yachts. Most of the hotels and motels, particularly popular with students during college vacations, are built opposite the beach and separated from it by the coastal road. You can park your car in sight of the waves and make forays to restaurants across the highway.

trams pulled by a jeep. Guides give informative commentaries during the tour past sumptuous waterfront homes, the car museum, the petting zoo, orange groves, and the Seminole Village where you can buy trinkets and see alligator wrestling. Join the train at your hotel; ask the hotel bell-captain for information.

Ocean World on S.E. 17th Street entertains with dolphin and sea-lion shows, a tank of sharks, displays of turtles, reef fish, alligators, caged monkeys and macaws. Across 17th Street from Ocean World lies Port Everglades, a major terminal for cruise-ships and freighters. If you head for the ocean along the A1A from here, you'll come to **Bahia Mar,** an attractive marina with its own club, pool and restaurant.

Sightseeing boats from Miami Beach stop over in Fort Lauderdale, and a Mississippi River paddle-boat, the 550-passenger *Jungle Queen*, embarks each evening for a 4-hour cruise with music, food and fun. Another riverboat, the *Paddlewheel Queen*, holds 400 passengers on three decks and takes daytime cruises to the mangrove swamps, leaving each afternoon from the pier a block south of Oakland Park

Fort Lauderdale has been on the upswing for some time. Morale is high and people are friendly. They're openly dismissive of the various titles given to the city such as "Venice of America", "Tennis Capital of the World", "Yacht Capital" or "Co-ed Capital". Healthy looking visitors throng the beaches, and the canals buzz with pleasure craft.

To get acquainted with the town, view the sights from rubber-wheeled sightseeing

ORLANDO | FORT PIERCE

PALM BEACH

West Palm Beach

Palm Springs — Lake Worth

Atlantis — Lantana
— Hypoluxo

Boynton Beach — Ocean Ridge
— Gulf Stream

Golf — Delray Beach

Highland Beach

Boca Raton

Deerfield Beach

Lighthouse Point

Pompano Beach

Tamarac — Sea Ranch Lakes
Oakland Park
Lauderhill — Wilton Manors
Coral Springs
Sunrise
Plantation
Hacienda Village — **FORT LAUDERDALE**

Davie — Dania

West Hollywood — **Hollywood**
— Hallandale

Pembroke Park — Golden Beach

North Miami — North Miami Beach

Bal Harbour
Surfside
North Bay Village

Miami Beach

MIAMI

LAKE OKEECHOBEE, FORT MYERS

FLORIDA'S TURNPIKE (TOLL)

MIAMI INTERNATIONAL AIRPORT

KEY WEST

ATLANTIC OCEAN

N

0   5   10 km
0   5 miles

GOLD COAST

Beach Bridge. On the evening cruise, the boat follows a 25-mile route down the Intracoastal Waterway. The tour includes a charcoal-steak dinner and a live band provides dance music.

Sharing Fort Lauderdale's attractions, POMPANO BEACH boasts its own paddle-boat, plus horse racing in Pompano Park.

For a quieter resort town try BOCA RATON. As many people fish off the beach here as take to the waves. The public beaches hidden behind tropical dunes have rest-rooms, showers, and long expanses of hot sand. One of these places, Spanish River Park, has a picnic ground with tables. Boca claims to be the "Winter Polo Capital of the World" and the sport is played regularly on Sundays between January and April.

North past the high-rise condominiums and golf clubs of DELRAY BEACH brings you to **Lake Worth.** Casino Park Beach, a public beach of sloping sand next to Kreusler Memorial Park, boasts a surfing tide, rest-rooms and show-

Even in expensive Palm Beach window-shopping is still free.

ers. A fast-food restaurant, a shop and a place to rent rod and reels are set up on the short fishing pier. The park has picnic tables, barbecue-pits and a children's playground under the palms. The municipal swimming pool stands alongside a row of stores selling swimsuits and craft items.

Beautiful Italianate homes hide behind the walls and clipped hedges of **Palm Beach,** one of America's wealthiest communities. Some of the houses crowded along the 5-mile strip of land are boarded up while their owners practise their professions in the great American cities. But others are rented to tourists. Drive through to admire the landscape gardening, but don't stop. Loitering may attract the attention of the alert police force. Stroll along **Worth Avenue** (see also p. 90) amid nostalgic Mediterranean-style buildings from the 1920s with palm-filled courtyards, elegant

These unusual Floridians are natural friends at feeding-time.

shops and restaurants. Don't miss the **Henry Morrison Flagler Museum.** The extravagant mansion retains some original furniture and a display of photographs giving interesting insights into the Florida of the railroad era. (Henry Flagler was the enterprising 19th-century businessman who built the railroad, see p. 19.)

WEST PALM BEACH, across the causeway, is a more accessible resort with motels stretching along the highway. The **Norton Gallery of Art** on US 1 displays a permanent exhibition of art, a splendid collection of jades and temporary exhibits featuring all the current trends on the New York scene. Plays straight from Broadway come to spend the winter at the Royal Poinciana Playhouse. For beaches go south to Lake Worth (see above) or north to RIVIERA BEACH.

From West Palm Beach, the causeway at Blue Heron Boulevard leads across to Palm Beach Shores, a new development of hotels and motels incorporating a variety of leisuretime facilities. JUNO BEACH and JUPITER BEACH to the north, though lacking in nightlife, have a relaxed and charming atmosphere.

If you're an animal lover, take the highway inland to **Lion Country Safari.** Here you can drive your car through herds of lion, elephant, giraffe, zebra, and ostrich, or ride on the miniature steam railway.

The area known as the Gold Coast comes to an end at West Palm Beach. But for aficionados of the ocean, the Florida coast continues for another 300 blissful miles to the state line.

West Palm Beach to St. Augustine

Once a mangrove swamp with offshore sandbars, the entire coast is a long, long island separated from the mainland by a saltwater strip called Indian River or Indian Creek. The leisurely route via A1A progresses through the seaside resorts, frequently crossing bridges where Indian River is connected to the ocean by inlets.

The Jonathan Dickenson State Park, 13 miles south of STUART, provides vacation cabins, hookups for campers and the usual facilities for fishing, swimming, boating, canoeing and hikes along nature trails. Between FORT PIERCE and MELBOURNE, sand dunes, shell shops, boutiques, motels and the occasional steakhouse are the main features of the landscape.

Further north, MERRITT ISLAND protrudes into the Atlantic. It was from here, on an area of the island called Cape Canaveral, that the first man was launched to the moon in 1969. Don't miss a visit to the **John F. Kennedy Space Center.** (You might even be lucky enough to be there on a launch day. You can call toll-free 43

[1-800-432-2153] to find out when launches are scheduled.) The Visitor Center belonging to the spaceport is just off the NASA Causeway linking A1A and US 1. Multimedia shows and exhibits of all descriptions will help you unravel the amazing technology of putting men into space. Among other items on display is a small lump of real moon rock, whose value (due to the limited supply) is considered higher than any mineral or precious metal found on earth.

On the bus tour (which may vary for operational reasons), you'll be shown the highlights of the Man on the Moon programme of the late 1960s including the gigantic VAB (Vehicle Assembly Building), the moon launch pad and Mission Control. Allow at least half a day to admire the fascinating displays.

Some 60 miles north of Cape Canaveral lies the "World's most famous Beach", as **Daytona** is known. The resort is one of the most popular with vacationers from up north. It has a desperate and well-used look. Hotels and motels with twitching, red neon bid against each other in their offers of lower prices. Daytona is a bargain city. There are restaurants that might offer you a Coke for 10 cents and a hamburger in a bun for a quarter. But the Coke is half water and the hamburger may leave a lot to be desired. It is a motorcyclist's town, with leather and chrome Hell's Angels trundling through the streets at ominous speeds.

The best feature of Daytona is its hard-packed 23-mile long sand **beach,** which doubles as a road. (Every few weeks a stalled car gets caught by the high tide.) The flat beach and shallow water are ideal for children, and the many lifeguard towers make it a safe place for them to bathe. Just south, near New Smyrna Beach is the inlet where Ponce de León, the discoverer of Florida, came ashore. If he were to arrive today, no doubt he would be nonplussed by the nearby city, with its motorcycle cultists and their heavy machines.

On July 4 each year, the annual 400-mile stock-car race is held at the **Daytona International Speedway.** A better-known race, the Daytona 500, is usually scheduled for late February. An entire car and

Daytona's hard-packed sand is perfect for tandem bike touring.

44

motorcycle culture has grown up around the track with parades, flea-markets and special events. Elsewhere the high-riding and low-riding hot-rodders cruise the streets, racing along the strip, or peeling out from the traffic lights.

Drive 20 miles inland from ORMOND BEACH (just north of Daytona), to get to LAKE GEORGE and Ocala National Forest. Off Highway 40 at JUNIPER SPRINGS, warm water surges out of the ground to form a natural swimming pool. There are other spa-resorts, notably ALEXANDER SPRINGS to the south of the forest and the widely known **Silver Springs**

on its western edge. Here you can view a menagerie of animals from a safari boat, or admire fish and underwater plants through the floor of a glass-bottomed boat. Elsewhere on the grounds are a reptile institute, water-slides and a collection of antique cars.

The **Ocala National Forest** itself—a sizable wilderness of lakes, hills and springs—offers first-class camping, hiking and fishing. To the west is the town of OCALA and nearby "Six Gun Territory", a family-orientated attraction that recreates the atmosphere of a cowboy and gold-mining town. North-west of the forest is the university city of GAINSVILLE. Back on the coast more oceanariums with dolphins leaping and whales soaring into the air can be found at **Marineland**.

Some 18 miles north of Marineland, **St. Augustine** is the oldest city in the United States (founded 1565). Spanish architecture, beautiful churches and a distinctly colonial atmosphere make a change from Florida's "Worlds", "Jungles" and aquaria.

The most interesting building is the **Castillo de San Marcos,** a Spanish fortress completed in 1695. The fortified walls are up to 12 feet thick in places. Exhibits and recreations of the historical events connected with the fort are presented daily.

A sightseeing train will take you on a general tour of the historic old city, and then you can return to favoured attractions such as the Oldest House or the **Oldest Store Museum.** This turn-of-the-century emporium is stocked with thousands of fascinating

and authentic items from that period, many of them accidentally discovered in a warehouse attic. You can see old buttoned shoes and lace corsets, toys, dolls, groceries, medicines, bonnets, bicycles, hats, guns and many other things. **Potter's Wax Museum** provides continuous lecture tours which lead through an enormous collection of historic figures in tableaux. The **Lightner Museum** has an interesting collection of Victorian and 19th-century musical instruments.

On summer evenings at the St. Augustine amphitheatre, the founding of the city is re-enacted in the outdoor pageant, "Cross and Sword".

Boats in Silver Springs cruise amid jungle flora and fauna. Natural beauty here remains unchanged since the days of the conquistadores.

Walt Disney World

The world's single most popular tourist attraction, Walt Disney World, lies 20 miles southwest of Orlando (see p. 61) off Interstate 4 and U.S. Highway 192. Millions of people come to enjoy themselves here every year. More than just a colourful theme park, Walt Disney World is actually an immense holiday resort development with its own hotels, campgrounds, golf courses, swimming and boating facilities, even blocks of vacation villas and shops. All in all, the site covers some 28,000 acres—an area roughly twice the size of Manhattan Island.

Visitors to Walt Disney World generally divide their time between the 100-acre theme park known as the Magic Kingdom and the nearby theme attractions of Epcot Center, spread out over a further 260 acres. Several tour companies operate excursions to the Magic Kingdom and Epcot Center—your hotel or any travel agent can give you full details on what's available.

During peak periods, it's important to arrive early in the morning. In high season (July, August and all national holidays), the crowds may literally fill the park to overflowing by early afternoon, and the entrance gates may be closed.

The attractions or rides last five to 15 minutes or so. Access is controlled, but huge numbers of people can be accommodated—as many as 60 a minute or 2 to 3,000 an hour. Don't be afraid to queue up on lines that seem impossibly long. You may beat the crowds by visiting the Magic Kingdom in the morning and Epcot later in the day; start with the attractions most distant from the entrance gates and work your way backwards.

To gain a fair impression of the Magic Kingdom and Epcot Center, you have to spend at least two days at Disney World.

The Magic Kingdom

From the Ticket and Transportation Center, take the ultramodern monorail or an old-time ferryboat across the vast man-made lake. Whichever you choose, you'll arrive at the entrance to the Magic Kingdom in only a few minutes.

Walk through the entrance and you'll find yourself in the middle of a fairyland dominated by Cinderella's storybook castle. Walt Disney, creator of Mickey Mouse and maker of innumerable cartoons and adventure movies, planned just **49** such a place for all his fantasies to come to life. All the characters are here, in settings which instantly recall Disney movie scenes. The Magic Kingdom is divided into six different sections. Stroll from one "land" to the next slowly—there's a lot to see and do.

Main Street, USA. As you entered the Magic Kingdom, you passed beneath the Main Street Railroad Station, an authentic replica of the buildings which were every town's centre of attraction in the Age of Steam. Before you lies Main Street, USA, first of the six "lands" in the Magic Kingdom. Gabled and turreted turn-of-the-century buildings line both sides of Main Street and surround the Town Square. City Hall, to your left, is the place to go for detailed information about any aspect of the Magic Kingdom or Walt Disney World.

The square is always filled with life. Roaring-Twenties musicians draw a crowd to the cinema, bespectacled tellers count out bills at the bank, and waitresses in long dresses move briskly from table to table in the Town Square Café. Soon you'll see an antique double-deck bus chug up the street, passing an even older horse-drawn tram-car.

It will take some time to make your way down Main Street. You'll find yourself stopping continually to admire the brightly painted houses and stores, or to duck into the old-fashioned Ice Cream Parlor. The cinema screens films all day long (there is no admission charge). You may also want to spend an hour in the Penny Arcade, where flicker-picture and stereoscope shows recall a bygone era. Main Street is not all entertainment, though. The various shops sell everything from tobacco to hand-blown glass, from jewellery to ladies' hats. Restaurants and cafés can satisfy your yearning for anything from a quick hot dog to an elaborate meal.

At the end of Main Street, USA, over a bridge, is a circular plaza backed by Cinderella Castle, the central 18-storey symbol of the Magic Kingdom. You can take any one of the routes leading to the different "lands" from here. Our description proceeds in a clockwise fashion, on the road to Adventureland.

Adventureland. Exotic tropical flora and fauna fill the cool glades and sun-baked trails of Adventureland. First you'll spot the gigantic banyan tree which supports the Swiss Fam-

Hungry or not, the smell of hot, fresh popcorn is irresistible.

ily Robinson Treehouse. For all its woody authenticity, it's a surprise to learn that the "tree" is actually made of concrete. Just beyond are the rough-hewn riverside shelters from which you board motor launches for the Jungle Cruise. Waterfalls, trailing vines, hostile natives from a variety of cultures, and surprisingly realistic "wild animals" meet your boat at every turn. From the Spanish-style Caribbean Plaza, branch off on an adventure to hear enchanted Tiki birds sing **51** in the Tropical Serenade. Or, in the opposite direction, join Pirates of the Caribbean for a voyage to their treasure trove.

Frontierland. America's frontier history, both real and legendary, fills Frontierland. Have a snack at Pecos Bill's Café, take aim at the old-time Shootin' Gallery, or laugh at the Country Bear Jamboree. At some moment during your visit to Frontierland, you're sure to hear the whistle of a riverboat coming round the bend. Jump on one of these elegant triple-deckers for a short cruise or just make the quick hop across the river to Tom Sawyer Island on a Tom Sawyer raft or a keelboat. Before leaving the Old West, see if there's a free seat at the Diamond Horseshoe Revue. But if you want to be sure of getting in, reserve seats at the revue early in the morning.

Liberty Square. From Frontierland, it's only a few steps to Liberty Square, fourth of the "lands" in the Magic Kingdom. Cowboy songs fade away to be replaced by the trill of "Yankee Doodle", and the architectural style changes from Old West to New England. If it's time for lunch, the Liberty Tree Tavern will keep you in the proper colonial frame of mind during a full meal.

Snacks and soft drinks are on sale at The Fife and Drum.

The Hall of Presidents is a major attraction in Liberty Square, with America's great leaders brought to life through "Auto-Animatronics". Even though you know for sure that the performers are mechanical replicas, the moment will come when you'll actually believe you're listening to Washington and Lincoln. Your adventure in The Haunted Mansion nearby will mix phantoms and fantasy, fright and frivolity into a memorable few minutes that seem like an hour.

Fantasyland. The Magic Kingdom is pure fantasy throughout, but Fantasyland is the most fantastical. Remember Captain Nemo's sinister submarine in *20,000 Leagues Under the Sea?* Here you can board a replica for an underwater voyage. At the Mad Hatter's Tea Party, take a dizzying whirl in a gigantic teacup. Children will love the trip through the dark forest to meet Snow White's Seven Dwarfs—and the Wicked Witch. Mickey Mouse, Peter Pan, Dumbo the Flying Elephant, and the reckless Mr. Toad from *Wind in the Willows* are all hosts to different adventures in Fantasyland. But the most graceful and yet exhilarating ride here is Cinderella's Golden Carousel, a classic merry-go-round with gleaming brass, glittering lights and cheerful music.

From Fantasyland, you can take the Skyway cablecar on an airborne ride to Tomorrowland. If you'd prefer to walk, choose a route that passes Cinderella Castle, and stop in for a look. The passageway within the castle is lined with surprisingly fine mosaics portraying scenes from the Disney film *Cinderella*. In the chambers to each side of the passageway are King Stefan's Banquet Hall and The King's Gallery, a gift shop.

Tomorrowland. The Magic Kingdom's glance at things-to-come is Tomorrowland, sixth and last of the Kingdom's "lands". See what it would be

Mouse known to millions: Minnie, Mickey's girlfriend, chats with everyone in the Magic Kingdom.

like to take part in a Mission to Mars, or to pilot a StarJet into outer space. The imposing white mass of steel, visible throughout the Kingdom, is the Space Mountain. Inside it are displays of RCA space-age technology, and a terrifying rollercoaster ride which simulates a race through space. Be sure to heed the sinister warning-signs, don't attempt the ride if you've got a weak heart or a delicate stomach. The race through space is a bashing, bone-jangling experience rather than a gentle glide. Instead, find your way to the WED-Way People Mover, a revolutionary system of transport. The WEDWay's little cars float on a cushion of electromagnetic force, with never a bump or bruise.

Several attractions in Tomorrowland are open to everyone for free, sponsored by large companies. Lines for the free attractions tend to be short, and the shows are well worth the time spent—there's never a hard sell. From Tomorrowland, the road leads back to Cinderella Castle, and down Main Street, USA, to the Kingdom entrance.

Before leaving the Magic Kingdom, why not take a last look by climbing aboard the Walt Disney World Railroad?

The circular track surrounds the entire 100 acres of the Magic Kingdom, but the journey takes less than a quarter-hour. The four narrow-gauge steam locomotives which haul the open passenger cars are the real thing. Built by Baldwin of Philadelphia in the 1920's they were discovered, still hard at work, in the wilds of Mexico's Yucatan Peninsula in 1960. After complete restoration, they began their new life in the Magic Kingdom.

Epcot Center

Twenty years in the making, Walt Disney World's vaunted "Experimental Prototype Community of Tomorrow" is not a town at all, but rather an educational theme park chock-a-block with attractions that enlighten and entertain. You won't forget for a minute that Disney "imagineers" are at work here. A sophisticated array of special effects and computerized gadgetry, including audio-animatronics (three-dimensional animated figures), enliven the proceedings in two distinct theme areas: Future World and World Showcase. What is more, some of America's most prestigious corporations are in on the act. General Motors, Exxon and Kodak among others serve as consultants and sponsors for various shows.

Situated 2½ miles from the Magic Kingdom, Epcot is accessible via a monorail line.

Future World

Following on the success of the Magic Kingdom and its many lands, the Disney organization conquers new territory at Future World—the realms of communications, transport, agriculture, energy and creativity. Travel back in time on the vertiginous **Spaceship Earth*** ride and view scenes depicting the development of communications. After spiralling high into the geodesic dome that symbolizes Epcot, you're swept down at last to Earth Station, the visitor information center.

Straight ahead lie the twin buildings of **Communicore*,** where exhibits elaborate on the communications theme. Hear the latest regional and international news at the Electronic Forum and participate in the Epcot poll, a survey of public opinion. Watch the "Astuter Computer Review", a look behind the scenes at the role of computers in Disney World operation. Or learn about experimental communications systems at Futurecom.

Grouped around Communicore are further attractions of Future World. Don't miss the Exxon-sponsored **Universe of Energy** show, presented in a unique travelling theatre; the seats actually move, powered by solar cells on the roof of the building. A spectacular film (about energy sources, of course) is followed by a trip through stage sets dramatizing the formation of fossil fuels, complete with audio-animatronics dinosaurs and primaeval mist.

The General Electric Corporation presents **Horizons,** a voyage into the future. Destinations include a farm where robots harvest crops and a colony in outer space where people play zero-gravity baseball.

The **World of Motion** (General Motors) brings the history of transport to life in a series of vignettes that spans the gap from the cave-man era to the city of tomorrow. Even babies enjoy the ups and downs of this ride-through spectacle, featuring a whimsical recreation of Leonardo da Vinci's studio and "the world's first traffic jam". On view in the Transcenter is a round-up of GM's latest models.

---

*If the crowds here overwhelm you, come back after 3 p.m. or so.

exhibit, which features an underwater "seacab" ride through the biggest artificial coral reef in the world, stocked with sundry specimens of marine life, from dolphins to barracuda. The underwater restaurant here is pretty spectacular, too.

The pavilion sponsored by Kraft foods focuses on **The Land**. A boat ride, "Listen to the Land", is on offer here. Cruise past more audio-animatronics sets and on through an experimental garden created with the help of the University of Arizona. The plants—"real and alive", as the guide proclaims—flourish in sand, suspended from growing frames, floating in water. Not a particle of soil nor a sign of decay contaminates this futuristic Eden. (Walking tours are available to those who sign up in the morning.)

World Showcase

Beyond Future World, ranged around the perimeter of a man-made lagoon, stand the great monuments of the world in all their Disney-replicated glory. The "imagineers" have clearly had a field day here. A scale model of the Eiffel Tower rises high above the Florida landscape (but not quite high enough), and a di-

Two audio-animatronics characters, Dreamfinder and his cohort Figment, a friendly dragon, lead the way on Kodak's **Journey into Imagination.** An explosion of special effects insures the popularity of this show, in celebration of creativity.

You'll enjoy the **Living Seas**

Walt Disney Production/Epcot Center.

Walt Disney Production/Epcot Center.

minutive version of Venice's famed Campanile nestles alongside a compact Doges Palace. Disney also brings you Peking's Temple of Heaven, a Mayan pyramid, a pastiche of a medieval German village, and so on. However small the scale it's all much larger than life. And all the more fun for that. To Disney World's credit, people unfamiliar with the originals claim they'd like to compare them with the copies, rather than the other way around.

Epcot's "Land" pavillion and Spaceship Earth.

But the monuments are just one aspect of World Showcase. Each country exhibit aims to present typical aspects of a culture and its cuisine. Listen to German Alp horn players, watch a French mime, enjoy an honourable approximation of pasta specialities at the Disney World affiliate of a well-known restaurant in Rome. While you're at it, take in a bit of China (see a circlevision film on the country), Japan (shop in a branch of the Mitsukoshi department store) and the United Kingdom (a Pearly band provides entertainment and cashmeres and kilts are offered for sale).

The centrepiece of World Showcase is, naturally, the American pavillion, a Colonial Georgian-style edifice. (Attribute it to patriotism or chauvinism, as you please.) In the American Adventure show (a "must-see"), scenes from U.S. history are re-enacted by audio-animatronics characters. And there's more to come; World Showcase is expanding to include Spain, Israel and Equatorial Africa.

To promote authenticity and international understanding, a certain number of foreign nationals are employed in each theme area. Ecological concerns also play a role in operations. Energy systems are pollution-free and there's an advanced waste-treatment system. But the most striking feature of both World Showcase and Future World is the overriding mood of optimism. The real world may be in sorry shape, but at Epcot, at least, there's hope for a better tomorrow.

Other Destinations

The heart of Walt Disney World is the Magic Kingdom and Epcot Center, but other fun-lands have their own unique attractions.

River Country is a mecca for splashy fun. Buy a day ticket (open in the evening; cheaper after 5 p.m.) and frolic on a lakeside beach where there are long, looping waterslides and white-water rapids for riding down on a tire. Take a dip in the heated swimming pool and swing on ropes and bridges. Across the water is **Discovery Island,** reached by boat, a nature sanctuary with walkways where you can admire the exotic plant and birdlife. There's also a walk-in aviary.

Vacation package plans are the best way to spend time at one of the fully equipped resort hotels. Golf, tennis, boating, swimming, restaurants serving a dozen exotic cuisines, and a vibrant nightlife are the attractions.

The Walt Disney World Village at LAKE BUENA VISTA, at the edge of Buena Vista, Lagoon, has shops, rental villas and its own golf club.

On the south side of Seven Seas Lagoon, the longhouses of the Polynesian Village Resort Hotel lie hidden among the palm trees. South Seas cuisine is featured on restaurant menus. On the grounds there are pools and waterfalls as well as sandy lake-side beaches. The monorail connects you with the Magic Kingdom.

The giant vaulting-horse of a building with the monorail running through it is the Contemporary Resort Hotel. With over 1,000 rooms, the resort is served by several restaurants, a huge games room, boutiques and tennis courts equipped with a video tennis clinic. The hotel is on the shores of Bay Lake, the site of Contemporary Resort Marina and a variety of swimming pools. At night-time there is a cinema (Disney movies), floorshows

Seconds before splashdown, at River Country's slippery slide.

Disney World Details

Banks. Branches in the Magic Kingdom and at Epcot Center (open daily 9 a.m. to 4 p.m.) offer a variety of services, including currency exchange, the cashing of personal cheques, transfer of funds, etc.

Children. Baby Care Centers provide excellent facilities for changing and feeding infants. The names of lost children are registered here.

First Aid Centers. Emergency medical assistance is provided in the Magic Kingdom (near Crystal Palace) and at Epcot Center (behind Odyssey Restaurant).

Guided Tours. Offered outside peak periods at Epcot Center and in the Magic Kingdom.

Lockers. Situated at several locations in the Magic Kingdom, Epcot Center and the Transportation and Ticket Center.

Lost and Found. Reclaim lost property at the main Lost and Found Station (tel. 824-4245). Ask any Disney employee about the whereabouts of lost children.

Pets. Animals are not allowed in the Magic Kingdom or Epcot Center. They will be cared for in one of the Walt Disney World kennels at a modest charge.

Photography. Borrow a camera (deposit required; you supply the film) at Camera Centers in the Magic Kingdom or Epcot Center. Flash equipment may not be used indoors.

Pushchairs and Wheelchairs. Available for hire (nominal charge).

Restaurant reservations. Booking for dinner at one of Epcot Center's World Showcase "table service" establishments can be made in person only at Earth Station (Spaceship Earth). Book early in the morning during peak periods. Reserve for lunch in person at the establishment itself.

Tickets. *One-day tickets* are good for entry either to the Magic Kingdom or Epcot Center and all rides and exhibits. Not valid on monorail, ferry boat or bus. For same-day readmission, ask the guard at the exit to stamp your hand with an invisible code. The *World Passport* (3-, 4- and 6-day; 1 year) admits holders to Magic Kingdom, Epcot Center and all rides and exhibits. Includes unrestricted use of Walt Disney World transport system, plus (6-day and 1-year passports) free parking. For prices, see page 105.

Visitor Information. Brochures, maps and mini-guides are distributed in the Magic Kingdom (City Hall) and at Epcot Center (Earth Station, Spaceship Earth).

and an orchestra for dancing. The resort also has its own health spa.

The Golf Resort Hotel overlooks the Magnolia and Palm golf courses where the Walt Disney World National Team Championship Golf Classic is played. There are putting greens, driving ranges, tennis courts and a pool.

Beside Bay Lake and under the trees is a 640-acre resort with campsites for your trailer, camper or motorhome. In the Fort Wilderness Campground, you can rent a trailer if you haven't got your own, or camp in a tent. Fort Wilderness includes River Country, and you'll have access to many hiking and biking trails. Two "trading posts", or stores, provide food, and a real steamtrain will take you on a long loop around the property. You can rent horses for the trails as well as boats for the lake.

For more information, contact Walt Disney World, Box 40, Lake Buena Vista, Florida 32830, USA; telephone (305) 824-4321. For vacation package information, contact the Walt Disney World Central Reservations Office, P.O. Box 78, Lake Buena Vista, Florida 32830. In England, write to Walt Disney Productions, 31 Soho Square, London W1.

Central Florida

Busy, cosmopolitan **Orlando,** the largest city in central Florida, entered the tourist sweepstakes when Disney World moved in down the road. The overflow of visitors packs the city, swelling the hotels and filling the tills. Orlando hosts the annual college football finals, held at the Tangerine Bowl, and offers plenty of other attractions to tempt families away from Mickey.

Sea World, a few miles out of town, puts on a fascinating show featuring performing dolphins, sea-lions, otters, penguins—and Shamu the killer whale. When you grow weary of the aquatic wonders, you can rest in the Japanese Village with its Japanese deer garden, or in the Hawaiian Punch Village. Sea World claims to have "more of everything", including several restaurants. You may want to check out Florida Festival, across the road, an enclosed, dining and entertainment complex.

Circus World lies a little south-west of Disney World. Barnum and Bailey's circus not only induces thrills and laughter, but it also invites participation. The kids can be clowns, the teenagers can try **61**

CENTRAL FLORIDA

the tight-rope and you can ride an elephant.

On a scorching day, there is nothing more tempting than **Wet 'n Wild,** also in the vicinity of Disney World. This collection of lakes and ponds is equipped with a variety of water-slides, bumper-boats, sailboats and other sports facilities. You can wander from one pool to another all day.

Among other diversions in the Orlando area are **Gatorland Zoo,** an alligator farm with turtles, monkeys, flamingoes and other tropical animals; **Reptile World Serpentarium,** containing an awesome array of lizards and snakes.

South of Orlando, the region of ranchland and citrus groves is roughly bounded by the towns of Lakeland, Bartow, Lake Wales and Haines City, and is within easy distance of Disney World, making it an ideal area in which to choose a base for excursions.

LAKELAND itself is a clean, neat city, with many fishing lakes and ponds. It is 20 miles from **Cypress Gardens,** an ornamental park surrounding a lake, open every day of the year. For one admission fee you can see four spectacular daily water-ski shows in which famous acrobatic skiers are towed along in a human pyramid. Within the Gardens are two theme areas: "Southern Crossroads", a replica of an old Southern town (circa 1900), and the Living Forest, a six-acre nature park where you can see reptile and exotic bird shows. Rides (electric boats cruise the waterways), shops and restaurants round out the possibilities.

The city of LAKE WALES emphasizes this region's affinities with the American Midwest by offering a winter home for the North Dakota Black Hills Passion Play. From February to April each year, the huge cast performs the last seven days in the life of Christ in an amphitheatre two miles out of town.

Just north of Lake Wales, **Masterpiece Gardens** is built around a mosaic replica of Leonardo da Vinci's *Last Supper.* The gardens have tame deer, a circular train ride, tight-rope bicycling parrots and performing ducks playing musical instruments. Another Lake Wales attraction, the **Bok Singing Tower,** is an elegant bell-tower set in a quiet garden. Every 30 minutes the bells play a "recital".

Flamingoes—a familiar sight in Florida. These are at Hialeah.

The Everglades

This watery plain is one of the most famous swamps in the world. It's a "river of grass" that flows almost imperceptibly from Lake Okeechobee, down through Florida and into the ocean.

The 1,400,000-acre **Everglades National Park** is a protected area of marshy land and broken coastline, policed by uniformed rangers. Winter, the dry season, is the ideal time to visit the Everglades. You'll see the greatest concentration of birdlife then and there are few mosquitoes. During the rainy summer months, the water level rises, animals retreat to high ground and insects multiply.

For maps and literature on the park, details of tours, activities and accommodation, write to Everglades National Park, P.O. Box 279, Homestead, Florida 33030.

From Miami follow the toll road south to HOMESTEAD, then take state road 27. Watch for signs indicating the way to the park. Just beyond Homestead (if you travel on US 1 instead of the toll road) you pass a line of inexpensive motels where you can spend the night unless you have booked accommodation in the park.

After a short drive, you come, first, to the park entrance and then to a **Visitor Center,** a place to buy film and to pick up a free, colourful map of the park, packed with information.

The park road runs 38 miles to the coast. Several marked turnoffs along the way take you out to campsites and picnic grounds beside lakes or near "hammocks"—raised areas in the swamps.

Home sweet home: alligators doze blissfully in the sunshine of Everglades National Park.

The first turnoff brings you to the **Royal Palm Visitor Center,** on the edge of a fresh-water slough (pronounced slew). Look down into the clear waters of the pond to see shoals of fish, including the Florida garfish, one of the principal foods of the alligator.

The auditorium here pro-jects regular, brief slide-shows on the Everglades, and the resident rangers will suggest where you should go. The Anhinga and Gumbo Limbo trails lead from this area.

The Anhinga Trail's raised boardwalk circles over the sawgrass marsh where you can see alligators, egrets, herons

and the anhinga, or snake-bird. This creature swims under water with its snake-like neck protruding, and then sits in a bush raising its wings to dry them. The Gumbo Limbo Trail is the other circular half-mile track through jungle vegetation. Keep your eyes open for raccoons, opossums, tree-snails and lizards. Between these two trails and the Flamingo Visitor Center, there are several other trails, sightseeing points, lakes and parking and picnic areas off the park road. The detailed map published by the National Park Service gives clear indication of all these facilities.

At the end of the main road, near the **Flamingo Visitor Center** is Flamingo, a fishing village on the shores of a shallow bay dotted with islands. It has had a colourful history as a centre of illicit ("moonshine") liquor production. Now life in the the small village revolves around a ranger station, a motel, housekeeping cabins and a campsite for recreational vehicles. A restaurant offers a lunch and dinner menu, and a grocery store provides for campers and picnickers.

Flamingo Marina has rental moorings or slips with hook-ups for electricity and water.

A small shop sells fuel, ships' stores and live bait. You can rent tackle, boats and canoes —even leave your laundry to be washed.

Take trips from Flamingo on sightseeing boats, or find your own way up to Everglades City through a chain of lakes and rivers called "The Wilderness Waterway". No hunting or firearms are permitted in national wildlife preserves, though you may catch and eat the fish. A licence is required for fresh-water fishing only. Tasty fish include trout, redfish, snapper and snook.

From the Flamingo observation deck, coin-operated telescopes are trained on flocks of great white herons, snowy egrets and roseate spoonbills which crowd the waters of the bay and decorate the trees of the islands like candles on a Christmas tree. While in the park, look out for otters, ospreys, Southern bald eagles and the Florida panther —rarest of all.

In summer, insects can be immobilizing (take *plenty* of insect repellent), and all the year watch out for poisonous plants (poison ivy, poisonwood and manchineel) and snakes (coral, water-mocassin, diamondback- and pigmy-rattler).

Be careful to respect the park regulations.

Another entrance to the park lies off the Tamiami Trail and provides a less demanding way to see the Everglades. Group tours operate from here. The trail is 100 miles long crossing the state from Miami to Naples on the west coast. Leave Miami on 8th St., and make sure to fill the tank before leaving town.

Signs all along the Trail promote rides, but COOPERTOWN is the centre for **airboat rides.** Flat-bottomed boats, powered by airplane propellers and equipped with benches will take you out in groups to slide over swamp and shoot between clumps of sawgrass, all the while belching blue smoke and roaring sufficiently to scare all the frogs out of the bog.

Stop at the **Miccosukee Indian Village,** farther on, to watch authentic crafts demonstrations and some honest-to-goodness alligator wrestling

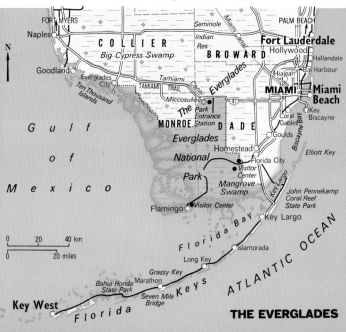

THE EVERGLADES

(braves vs. gators). A Creek people, the Miccosukees, have lived in isolation here since the time of the Seminole wars.

Beyond the village, the Tamiami Trail passes along the southern perimeter of the Big Cypress National Preserve, where the grey-barked trees standing over the swamp make for a landscape of desolation.

The western gateway to the Everglades is EVERGLADES CITY, the site of a ranger station and the terminus of a 100-mile inland route through the wilderness waterway for canoes and boats originating at Flamingo Visitor Center.

The Florida Keys

Curving westward from below Miami, the 100-mile scatter of islands called the Keys are stitched together by the world's longest ocean-going road. The **Overseas Highway** soars and leapfrogs out to the remote old naval town of Key West.

To get there from Miami, after Homestead follow Highway 1 south through 30 miles

Tourists speed through Florida swampland in an airboat. Giant turtles hide among the Keys.

of quiet swampland, where herons and storks glide across the road, their great untidy nests of sticks sitting atop poles. Without knowing it, you'll soon be on the first island, KEY LARGO, and close to the **John Pennekamp Coral Reef State Park,** an undersea area of tropical fish, sponges, reefs and wrecks. Water temperature is between 67°F and 85°F; and there are plenty of small shops which rent cameras, diving equipment and boats, as well as providing tuition. A glass-bottom boat makes regular departures along the reef for those who prefer to keep dry while admiring the fish.

Further down the Keys at the town of ISLAMORADA, you will find lots of diving competition and the biggest marina in the area. If you participate in the Islamorada Annual Fishing Tournament, you may catch a few of the estimated 600 species of fish in the surrounding waters. Here, too, is one of the oldest and one of the best marine shows in Florida. At the **Theater of the Sea,** engaging young trainers lead visitors from one rock-pool to another, pointing out dolphins, stingrays, sharks and sea lions.

At LONG KEY see Sea World's **Shark Institute,** with

the largest collection of sharks in the world, and at GRASSY KEY go to Flipper's Sea School, to view dolphins, rays, turtles, sharks and an alligator. Nearby is Aqua Dome Sea Life Exhibit, a tropical fish aquarium under a geodesic dome. The town of MARA-THON is a sizeable resort and crawfish fishing centre, with accommodation and restaurants. State parks with camping areas are to be found at Long Key and at **Bahia Honda,** which has a gorgeous tropical beach with cabanas.

When you have travelled the length of the Keys, you'll reach a remote little town which, some are predicting, may soon be as fashionable as Big Sur in California or Provincetown on Cape Cod.

⚓ Key West
The word "Key" comes from the Spanish *cayo* meaning a small island. It is possible that Key West was named Cayo Oesto by the discoverer of Florida, Ponce de León, who knew the island to be the most westerly of the chain. But for many years it was called Cayo Hueso, Bone Island, perhaps because a fierce battle with the Indians in the 18th century left the island littered with corpses.

But for all its violent past, Key West remains one of the friendliest towns in Florida.

This 1-by-3½-mile subtropical island is nearer to Havana than to mainland Florida. Its population is a balance of retired military personnel and their families, Cuban exiles, young people into health-foods and crafts, a black community with obvious West Indian musical connection, writers, painters and a gay community. The residents

are known as conchs (pronounced "konks"), after the king conchs which inhabit the waters offshore. These mollusks cling tenaciously to the undersea rocks. In the same stubborn manner, before the railway or highway were built, residents of Key West lived through several hurricanes, determined not to budge despite the poor communications and isolated life.

You approach the island via the newer, commercial quarter. Follow the road to the old town, and here you will find an odd collection of hotels and motels, often with heated pools under tropical palms. In Duval

Part of Key West's charm is in its well-preserved turn-of-the-century architecture. An easy way to see it all is on the Conch Tour train.

Street, full of shops and restaurants, you can visit **Sloppy Joe's,** one of the noisiest of the bars. Hemingway used to spend much of his time working here.

Duval Street terminates in **Old Mallory Square,** scene of Florida's best free show. Toward every sunset of every evening, a crowd gathers on this stone quay and entertains itself. You may see musicians, jugglers, fire-eaters, and eccentrics. The police move around exchanging good-natured insults with the street folk.

Close by Mallory Square stands the terminal of the Conch Tour Train, a mock railroad engine pulling a line of rubber-wheeled buggies. It takes you on a 14-mile trip past the island's sights including many fine wooden houses of a hundred years ago. The Old Town Trolley company competes for sightseers.

The **Ernest Hemingway House,** set in a lovely tropical garden, has a display of the writer's possessions. Legend has it that the scores of garden cats are descendants of his pets. Many of Hemingway's novels were written during the 30 years that he lived in Key West.

The famous painter and naturalist, John James Audubon, came to Key West in 1832 to paint the birds of the Florida Keys. The **Audubon House** where he lived has been restored and is open to the public. On view is a complete set of *Birds of America* and lovely old English furniture.

On Front Street wharf a replica of the Spanish treasure ship, the *Nuestra Señora de Atocha,* has bronze cannons and artefacts from a nearby wreck. Not far away is another sealife exhibition, the Turtle Kraals, home of 750-pound Big George, the largest turtle in captivity.

Key West, with its resourceful chefs, has a great many small and special restaurants serving original dishes at various prices. There are some very good craft shops offering leather, wood, cloth and ceramic gifts, and import shops stocked with low-priced oriental goods.

The intense sunshine here can be a problem for delicate skins, so take precautions against overexposure to the sun—even walking the city streets. Fortunately, Smathers Beach has the odd palm tree or two for shade. The living **coral reef** offshore breaks the waves making it unsuitable for surfing, but creating a haven for snorkellers.

The Gulf Coast

The west coast of Florida has a compelling similarity to southern California. The rapidly developing coastline between Naples and St. Petersburg has the same fresh towns gleaming white in the sun and commercial strips of drive-in businesses and shopping centres.

Much of the mainland coastline is protected by long, offshore sandbars, which means one must cross the salty lakes to find the beach. The coastline, from Marco Island near the Everglades up to Tampa, stretches for 178 miles with bays, inlets, lagoons, peninsulas and islands. The old fishing towns of this coast are being gradually eclipsed by new construction. At MARCO ISLAND and the town of GOODLAND, you can hire power-boats and sailboats and explore the "10,000 Islands" section of the Everglades. Many of the islets are wildlife sanctuaries, and you cannot go ashore.

The smart town of NAPLES has a famous shell-beach. A yacht will take you out to a small off-shore island for half a day of fishing or shell collecting. West of town, the African Safari Park features big-game animals and wild birds.

At BONITA SPRINGS, stop at Everglades Wonder Gardens to see all the creatures you might have missed in the Everglades. The ever-changing display may feature wildcats, eagles, snakes, owls, crocodiles, flamingoes, otters and deer. The National Audubon Society has preserved a sanctuary of 11,000 acres of wilderness at Corkscrew Swamp. A mile-long boardwalk passes through the great bald cypress trees.

Just before FORT MYERS you can visit the Edison Winter Home. America's "electrical wizard", inventor of, among many other things, the phonograph and the light bulb, Thomas Alva Edison (1847–1931), moved to Fort Myers for his health. He developed the present garden of exotic plants and trees in his search for new materials. The house contains his laboratory, a collection of old cars and phonographs and his study filled with personal effects.

Four miles north of Fort Myers, the Shell Factory is a museum and gift-shop that will entertain you for hours.

Towards the Gulf from North Fort Myers you will find Aquarama Waltzing Waters (fountains which play and move to music) plus a small lagoon featuring a dolphin, sea lion and water-skiing show.

Sandy-shoal islands or keys slightly north of Fort Myers include fashionable resorts like SANIBEL, site of the J.N. Darling National Wildlife Refuge, and CAPTIVA. Most exclusive of all is **Boca Grande** (accessible by toll bridge from ENGLEWOOD), long a favourite winter watering-hole for rich northerners. The village and surrounding shops are discreet and lowkeyed, a bastion of old-fashioned gracious living.

Venice, north again, claims fame as the winter headquarters of the Ringling Brothers Barnum and Bailey Circus, and **Sarasota** is the undisputed cultural capital of Florida. Art moved in surprisingly fast when John and Mable Ringling of circus fame established their **estate** here in the early 1920s. Within just a few years the couple built a Venetian-style palazzo and Italianate museum filled with hundreds of works of art that reflect not only the daring and flamboyance of the circus, but their own earnest striving for good taste—leaning towards the Italian Renaissance and Baroque.

The **Ringling Museum** displays several Rubens cartoons for the *Triumph of the Eucharist* cycle (the other two extant are in the Louvre in Paris).

Frans Hals, Lucas Cranach and Paolo Veronese are also represented in this excellent collection of 16th- to 18th-century paintings.

Near the museum is the **Asolo Theater,** a gem of Rococo architecture transported stone by stone from Asolo, north-west of Venice (Italy), and reassembled here. Visitors next head for **Ca'd'Zan** ("John's House" in Venetian patois), where the Ringlings' taste for the grandiose reigned supreme. The massive crystal chandelier came from New York's Waldorf-Astoria Hotel, while the oak and stained-glass bar was copied from the Cicardi Winter Palace in St. Louis, where John reportedly spent a good deal of time tippling with cronies. **The Museum of the Circus** on the estate grounds houses some lively memorabilia, of interest to circus buffs.

A nostalgic display of old cars, bicycles, antiques and musical instruments can be seen at **Bellm's Cars and Music of Yesterday,** just across Highway 41. At Sarasota's **Jungle Garden** you can feast your eyes on yet another beautiful botanical garden and zoo, stocked with a few jungle animals. Reptile and bird shows entertain the crowds daily.

Near the centre of Sarasota, the **Van Wezel Performing Arts Hall** is a popular venue for theatre, classical and jazz concerts. Dubbed the "purple people-seater", it rises beside the Gulf like a dramatic violet sail. The Frank Lloyd Wright team designed the building, completed in 1970.

Over the big causeway off Highway 41 lies Sarasota's prettiest shopping and restaurant centre, **St. Armand's Circle.**

Venice is the best place to look for a shark tooth souvenir.

Continuing up the coast to St. Petersburg, cross the impressive Sunshine Skyway, a toll bridge that soars high over the grey glitter of Tampa Bay. **St. Petersburg** is a quiet, safe kind of city, where motel and restaurant prices are reasonable. From the downtown area, you'll see a strange-looking inverted pyramid that seems to be floating in the water. It's **Pier Place,** a complex of shops with a restaurant on top.

A few blocks away, roam the **Sunken Gardens,** an astonishing tropical garden, where wild life and bird life congregate amidst bougainvillea and other exotic blooms.

Don't miss St. Pete's **Salvador Dali Museum** (1000 3rd Street South), donated to the city by a Cleveland industrialist. This is the world's largest collection of works by the Spanish surrealist, including paintings, sculptures, graphics and other objects valued at upwards of $35 million.

The long offshore island of **St. Petersburg Beach** can be reached by one of the three causeways. This modest strip is lined with hotels, motels, fast-food restaurants and shops. You can rent a boat and visit the islands in the mouth of Tampa Bay, and come back to a different restaurant each night.

Going north 10 miles you will find **Tiki Gardens,** a little Polynesian fantasy garden with shops and a restaurant. It is a short distance from Big Indian Rock Fishing Pier, where you can hire tackle and try your luck.

Across the wide bay by the expressway lies **Tampa,** a dynamic city which has distinguished itself in such sports as football (soccer). The Tampa Bay Rowdies introduce their games with good old-fashioned razzmatazz—leggy girls, bands and anything colourful and eye-catching to delight the crowds.

Many Cubans brought their cigar-making businesses up to the Latin quarter called Ybor City, popular for its Spanish restaurants and Latin music. The Anheuser-Busch Brewery has built an ornamental garden here that has grown into a major tourist attraction: **The Dark Continent (Busch Gardens),** an enormous African theme park, features giant aviaries, tropical gardens and a zoo. A monorail circulates through the park. The Adventure Island water park has

Tinkling fountains and cool arcades grace Ringling Art Museum.

beaches, waterfalls, waterslides and even waves. You are invited to tour the brewery and to sample the beer. You can also try the Python roller-coaster ride or the river rapids raft trip. Allow a full day to see Busch Gardens.

North of Tampa and St. Petersburg is TARPON SPRINGS, home of the sponge-diving industry. The industry was started by Greek immigrants at the beginning of the century and despite synthetic sponges is still going strong. At **Spongeorama** you'll be able to learn all about the history of sponges and visit various exhibits dedicated to the marine creature.

Thirty miles up the coast in the flamboyant tropical park of **Weeki Wachee,** admire the performing birds and wild animals, although the attraction is better known for its improbable underwater ballet. Maidens with flowing hair hold their breath, smile bravely and perform underwater acrobatics.

Another 3 miles north at HOMOSASSA SPRINGS, a boat ride will be fun; watch a hippopotamus yawn and admire the flamingoes.

Gulf Coast pleasures: a moment of suspense in Busch Gardens, a posh beach resort in "St. Pete".

Excursions

The best, cheapest and most exotically different excursion you can make from Florida is to the Bahamas*. Only 50 miles from Miami, these splendid tropical islands are scattered like pearls in an entrancing aquamarine sea.

The Bahamas is a self-governing nation which gained its independence from Britain in 1973 and, while American influence from the mainland is undeniable, the islands have an atmosphere all of their own. Best of all, for those who like peace and quiet, only 100 of the 700 islands in the archipelago are inhabited. So with a boat, a fishing line and a fridge full of iced drinks, your holiday will be made.

But for most people on an excursion from Florida, cruise-ships head for one or the other of the big ports: **Freeport** on Grand Bahama or **Nassau** on New Providence Island. Both of these cities provide plenty of shopping bargains. You can find British woollens at half the U.S. price, as well as many other good-quality products: Japanese cameras, china, crystal and French perfumes are all cheaper than in the United States. Local buys can make good souvenirs: shells, coconut-shell jewellery, rum, straw goods.

For one-day visitors to Nassau, a stroll around town will be worth the trouble. Some of the old houses date back to the early 18th century. The capital's straw market is a colourful spectacle that shouldn't be missed. Freeport offers the huge International Bazaar planned by a Hollywood set designer.

During the day, apart from the usual sports, diving is the most passionate of Bahamaian (and many tourists') pastimes. If you're staying overnight, casinos, restaurants and hotels will be just as eager to welcome you—and your dollars—as the shops during daytime.

Cruise-ships leave frequently for three- to four-day jaunts to the Bahamas (the ship is used as a hotel when in port). There's also a car-ferry connection between Miami and Freeport. Flights leave for Nassau and Freeport daily from a number of airports, in particular those serving Miami, Fort Lauderdale, West Palm Beach and Orlando.

* For vacationers planning an extended holiday to the Bahamas, the Berlitz BAHAMAS travel guide provides a comprehensive survey of all there is to see and do in the archipelago.

What to Do

Sports

With winter air like sparkling champagne and seas as clear as a tropical lagoon, Florida will have you out and playing before you can get your baggage unpacked.

Tennis, golf, shuffleboard, sailing, boating, canoeing, hiking, riding, hunting and fishing can all be found in Florida. There are also numerous spectator sports. Football, soccer, jai alai, baseball, polo, dog, horse and auto racing take place throughout the year. But of all these recreational pastimes, there's one activity that's more popular than any other...

Water Sports

Whether you prefer windsurfing, scuba-diving, waterskiing or just plain swimming, Florida's leisurely ocean waves and calm inland lakes have room enough for everybody.

Opportunities for scuba diving exist all along the Atlantic coast, but the best area is around the Florida Keys with its live coral reef and in the 20-mile-long John Pennekamp State Park (see p. 71).

Surfing and water-skiing are popular everywhere; windsurfing is also gaining ground. Local sea conditions are usually the determining factor for serious water sportsmen. Big waves mean surfing, small waves water-skiing or windsurfing. With a coastline as long as Florida's, beaches are legion—and often exceedingly lengthy (Daytona's, for instance, runs for 23 miles). There are quieter stretches on many of the islands off the west coast. Beaches on the Keys are generally rocky. Many public beaches have barbecue facilities, and it's well worth using them. A barbecued steak in the open air after a morning of strenuous swimming is nothing less than perfect.

Boating

Power-boats, sailboats and canoes are available for hire, as well as deep-sea fishing yachts manned by a captain. You can sail nearly everywhere. Some of the best power-boating is from Everglades City among the Ten Thousand Islands and down south in Florida Bay. Canoe routes go through the Everglades and down the rivers issuing from central Florida's springs and lakes.

Fishing

There are hundreds of different species of fish in the seas around Florida, and the piers, docks and marinas of the resorts are crowded with deep-sea fishing boats. Rods, reel and bait can be rented, and knowledgeable captains will help you get acquainted with the equipment. After that only patience will be necessary. Some boats go for the more certain mackerel and amberjack, but you can also try for the big ones—dolphin, marlin and shark.

Many resorts have a branch of F.I.S.H. (Florida Inland Sportsfishing Hosts), dedicated to making you a regular visitor to the local lakes and rivers. They publish brochures mapping the waters, listing accommodations, campsites, and fishing regulations. Okeechobee is best for lake fishing although big bass are also to be found in the St. Johns or Withlacoochee Rivers or in Lake

George. The canals are well-stocked and sometimes turn up saltwater fish such as tarpon or snook. The Education and Information Division of Florida's Department of Natural Resources provides information on boating and fishing. Write to 3900 Commonwealth Boulevard, Tallahassee, Florida 32303. Navigational charts are available at marinas and map dealers.

You'll need a visitor's licence if you plan to do freshwater fishing in Florida (available at marinas, tackle shops, etc.).

Golf

Golf is popular, cheap and available to all. There are around 40 courses in Greater Miami alone, as well as a heavy concentration of courses up the Gold Coast and around Palm Beach. You can gain access to many 18-hole courses for a few dollars. The local Chamber of Commerce will supply you with a brochure listing the courses.

Tennis

Tennis is an obsession in Florida. Most larger hotels have courts, many have teaching facilities and organize tournaments. Miami Beach has nearly 50 courts in two sep-

arate tennis centres. In Orlando try the clay courts of Orlando Tennis Club or the asphalt ones at the public club in Winter Park. Disney World's Contemporary Resort Hotel has a "tennis clinic" equipped with video equipment, practice lanes and automatic ball equipment. Anywhere in Florida you won't be far from a tennis club.

One tip: in summer, it's best to play early in the morning or late in the afternoon, before and after the relentless sunshine makes the humidity unbearable.

Hunting

Most tourists on a two-week jaunt to Florida don't come for the hunting scene. Nevertheless parts of northern Florida contain the best turkey shooting in the U.S.A. Rabbit, fox, raccoon and other small creatures can also be shot almost everywhere; deer is found in wilder districts.

Licences are necessary. Contact the Game and Freshwater Fish Commission for further details.

Spectator Sports

With its near-tropical winter climate, the state is the ideal place for northern baseball teams to keep fit during the winter. The Boston Red Sox, L.A. Dodgers, Baltimore Orioles and many other well-known American league teams find good weather in Florida.

Miami has its own football (American football) team, the Dolphins, whose home base is the huge **Orange Bowl stadium.** The Bowl doubles as the home of the University of Miami's "Hurricanes" football team. On January 1 each year two top collegiate teams meet in the Orange Bowl classic. Two hours before kick-off for any big game there is a park-and-ride service for visitors to the Bowl.

Florida hosts some fast-paced tennis tourneys, notably the Ilie Nastase Hamptons International, held in Miami in December.

As for professional golf, the prestigious Doral-Eastern PGA Open takes place in Miami every February or March.

In the greater Miami area three tracks ring the changes on the racing scene. (See the local press for dates of races.) Of the three, **Hialeah Park** attracts sightseers all year round thanks to its scenic surroundings. With its lake, beautiful-

Polo is just one of the many fast-paced spectator sports. A crafty bet might just pay off.

Calendar of Events

Few states can match the sheer number of special events held annually in Florida. For more detailed information, consult the local Chambers of Commerce.

January
: *Greek Festival* (Tarpon Springs). The Greek community of this west coast town celebrates its heritage.

  Three Kings Parade (Little Havana). A colourful spectacle, with bands, floats, marching units—the lot.

February
: *Silver Spurs Rodeo* (Kissimmee). A semi-annual orgy of calf-roping, steer wrestling and other feats of cowboy derring-do.

  Old Island Days (Key West). Conch-blowing contest, parades and other events commemorate the early history of the island.

  Speed Weeks (Daytona Beach). Two weeks of car races, including the celebrated Daytona 500.

  Big Orange Music Festival (Miami). Dade County—wide celebration, featuring every type of music from classical to rock.

  Grand Prix (Miami). Big names in the racing world compete on the streets of Biscayne Boulevard.

March/
April
: *Easter Sunrise Service* (Cypress Gardens). A worship service held at dawn on Easter Sunday.

July
: *U.S. Ocean Balloon Race* (Bahamas to Ft. Lauderdale). Balloonists from all over rise to the challenge of competition.

  Silver Spurs Rodeo (Kissimmee). February repeat.

  All-American Water-Ski Championship (Cypress Gardens). Watch the pros contend in Florida's water-ski capital.

September
: *Anniversary of the Founding of St. Augustine* (St. Augustine). Florida's oldest city recalls its past.

October
: *Hispanic Heritage Week Gala* (Miami). Art exhibits, lectures and other events are scheduled.

December/
January
: *Orange Bowl Festival* (Miami). Highlight is the nationally televised Orange Bowl Parade on New Year's Eve.

ly landscaped gardens and resident colony of flamingoes, the Park makes an unparalleled setting for the sport of kings. The other two sites are Calder Race Course just north of Miami and Gulfstream Park Race Track at Hallandale. Florida Downs Track at Tampa has a January to mid-March season. Horse racing also takes place at Gator Down Racing, Pompano.

Greyhound races are held at Daytona, Tampa, Palm Beach, Pensacola, Key West, Sarasota, Hollywood, St. Petersburg, Miami and Orlando.

Of the spectator sports activities available in Greater Miami, the most intriguing to a visitor is the Basque game of jai alai (pronounced 'hi li'). Fast and action-packed, jai alai is played at night in season, at the Biscayne Fronton in Miami, and at the Dania Fronton in the town of Dania (Broward County).

Finally, car and motorcycle racing at Daytona International Speedway near Daytona Beach attracts thousands of spectators; in February they gather for one of the world's famous races, the Daytona 500. Miami now has its own Grand Prix, a Monaco-style car race that takes place on Biscayne Boulevard.

Shopping

The ingenuity and competitiveness of American merchandising often provide some interesting bargains in goods you may find anywhere in the world. Before leaving home, check what you might need or crave in the way of household goods and electronic gadgets and make a note of the prices. In Florida you may find the same items, often with the very latest innovations, at much lower prices, especially at the discount stores advertised in the weekend editions of the local newspapers. Don't forget that American electrical products are designed to run on 110 volts. Make sure that what you buy can be adapted to your home voltage, if it's different.

As well as high quality electrical and manufactured goods and clothes, you'll find Indian handicrafts and a fascinating range of imports from Latin America and Asia.

Prices vary enormously from store to store. A bathing costume purchased at a seafront hotel boutique may be four times the cost of an identical one in a department store 200 yards away. So it pays to shop around.

For even better bargains, **89**

consult the local papers for sales. Most stores have them several times a year, usually closely following Christmas, Independence Day (July 4), Memorial Day, George Washington's or Lincoln's birthday and Thanksgiving.

A sales tax is charged on all purchases.

When and Where to Shop

Hours vary: suburban malls are open 7 days a week, 10 a.m. to 9 p.m., while shops in city centres are generally open only until around 5.30 p.m., closing on Sundays. Large chain-stores open on Christmas Eve, but not on Christmas Day, Easter Sunday, Thanksgiving and July 4.

In addition to the shopping malls, supermarkets, speciality shops, discount centres and chain stores familiar to all, the south-eastern seaboard of Florida has a style of shopping found only very rarely elsewhere: prestige malls.

The very buildings reflect the merchandise they contain, featuring tropical landscaping, modern sculpture and playing fountains, they are often innovatively designed by creative architects. Inside, you'll find the best of American designer boutiques, antique and jewellery shops and often branches

of such famous European houses as Charles Jourdan, Courrèges, Rodier, Gucci and Pucci. Even if the prices are out of your sight, the window-shopping will be a delight.

What to Buy

Florida keeps its eyes on Europe, New York and California, and is responsive to changes in fashion. Buy the latest in leisure-wear, bathing suits, robes, beach shoes, and patterned shirts. Many are attracted by the Bermuda shorts and colourful T-shirts emblazoned with provocative slogans which are on sale.

An intriguing find is a western store, selling leather goods and cowboy clothes. These stores actually supply real-life cowboys and ranchers, not just tourists, though the merchandise these days is not always U.S.-made. A well-fitting pair of chunky cowboy boots will last for years. At these stores you can get suede, fringed Indian jackets, jeans, silver belt buckles, leather hats and gloves and all manner of tooled purses, handbags, wallets and billfolds.

Some stores specialize in Indian crafts from all over America, including fine woven blankets, ponchos, wall hangings and skirts. You can bar-

Colourful patchwork garments are a speciality of Florida's Seminole Indian seamstresses.

gain for semi-precious jewellery, often turquoise stones set in silverwork. The prices may seem high, but judging by the huge increases in price over the last decade, you will be the owner of a beautiful and appreciating asset.

At import stores you'll find many unusual gifts to take back home. Attractive Oriental goods in woven raffia, wood, leather, metal and plastic are tempting, or go all the way and buy wicker furniture, rugs, pottery and lacquered umbrellas to send home.

America is the home of gadgets, kitchen aids, unusual toys and all kinds of mechanical or electronic wizardry. For real novelties, try a can of spray-cheese, or a miniature radio built into a pen, or one of those "executive toys" which sit on your office desk and tick away the afternoon. There are bargains in digital watches, calculators and portable typewriters—many of them imported, but often cheaper in America.

And finally you can send back a box of good old Florida sunshine. One of the larger roadside fruitstands will pack their own tangerines, oranges, grapefruit or a mixture of fruit and have it shipped home for you, see also p. 102.

see also p. 102.

Nightlife

At sunset Florida slides happily into the world of the Caribbean. In Miami, the dominant note is Cuban, the exiles showing the more staid locals what, for better or for worse, Havana was like before the revolution. Cuban supper-clubs raise

the temperature with flamenco dancing, Spanish guitars and castanets. After a couple of rum-laced cocktails, the Latin fantasies take over.

Miami and Miami Beach also have an endless kaleidoscope of girlie shows and "naughty" French (or naughty "French") revues and some intriguingly sleazy drag-queen shows.

Tours of the night clubs are organized from the hotels in limousines or buses, offering a package that includes cocktails at one club, dinner at another and a floorshow or other entertainment elsewhere. If you prefer to go off on your own, Miami also has dozens of piano-bars with their wistful mixture of soft lights and sweet music, even a trio or two for a quiet spot of cheek-to-cheek dancing. It's coming back, or perhaps it never went away.

Broadway musical comedies send road-shows to Miami Beach, Fort Lauderdale or Coconut Grove. That special American institution, the dinner-playhouse, where you can get a meal and a play, neither of them too heavy, is available at Fort Lauderdale and Tampa.

Concerts classical and pop take place year-round at the Miami Beach Theater of the Performing Arts and, in Miami, at Gusman Center of the Performing Arts and the Convention Center across from Du Pont Plaza. Dade Country Auditorium is the venue for a season of opera in winter.

Key West specializes in casual live music in its bars and cafés—jazz, rock'n'roll, country and western—especially along Duval Street. The bands are of good quality and seem to play at all hours of the day and night. The Tennessee Williams Playhouse, as its name might suggest, offers drama of a little more demanding quality than the musical comedies up the coast.

If you're slowing down, you might like the nostalgic music of the big lush orchestras that give concerts in St. Petersburg. Occasionally a supper-club there will race the blood of the local inhabitants in their sunset years with some upbeat calypso music, but most often it's nice and easy.

If you find yourself around Fort Lauderdale in the early spring, especially in the weeks leading up to Easter, you can't

Surrealistic window display graces Florida shopping mall.

93

miss the astounding spectacle of the annual spring rites of the students surging down from New England and the Middle West in search of the sun. From earliest evening the bars all along "the Strip" of Atlantic Boulevard and inland on the Federal Highway are crammed full of lobster-pink rip-roaring revellers hell-bent on having a good time. They create their own entertainment much of the time with impromptu dancing, singing and clowning, but they're helped out occasionally with deafening rock 'n roll bands. Round about midnight begin the contests: wet T-shirt beauty contests for the girls, go-go dancing by the boys, the judges being the ensemble of spectators of the opposite sex. See it to believe it. If you need a breath of more or less fresh air, there's another spectacle out on the Strip, the never-ending stream of carloads of boys and girls looking for each other—

sometimes, you feel, almost frightened to succeed. The supercharged atmosphere is perhaps the closest America gets to Saturnalia.

Then, as always, there's Disney World, where Orlando has cashed in on the fun for the kids with a stream of nightclubs, floorshows and girlie revues for the adults. The Disney organization provides every kind of all-American music—Dixieland, honkytonk, clean rock, folk music,

country and western. Exotica is at the other end of the monorail ride to Polynesian Village, where you can watch Tahitian hula dancing and even, perhaps, be inspired to go home and practice the Samoan sword dance with the bread knife and meat carver in the kitchen.

Take in the dazzle of Disney World or an exotic Gold Coast revue—that's entertainment.

Dining in Florida

Traditional American food with a light Latin accent—that's Florida cooking. Fresh seafood and local citrus products figure prominently on menus. You're also likely to happen on grits (resembles porridge), hush puppies (fried cornmeal balls) and gumbo (Creole stew with okra)—reminders that Florida is, after all, part of the South. The other major event, gastronomically speaking, is delicatessen food, the best outside New York. Where else can you find a Reuben—an improbable creation incorporating corned beef, Swiss cheese and sauerkraut grilled on kosher rye bread?

Meal Times
Florida restaurants keep fairly flexible hours. Breakfast is served from 7 to 11 a.m., lunch from about 11.30 a.m. to 1.30 p.m. and dinner from 5 or 6 to 9 or 10 p.m. Brunch is featured on Sundays between 11 a.m. and 3 p.m. Certain coffee shops open round the clock, and some restaurants offer an "early-bird special", a menu at a special price for diners who order their evening meal before 5 p.m. or thereabouts.

Where to Eat
Florida's eating houses range from informal lunch counters to elegant French restaurants with highly respected chefs. Dine indoors in air-conditioned comfort or eat outside with a view of sea, pool or tropical gardens; wherever you go, the emphasis is on informality.

Delicatessen restaurants specialize in gargantuan sandwiches made of corned beef, smoked tongue, turkey or roast beef, and many other fillings. Help yourself to the tempting array of relishes that are often placed on the table: sauerkraut, cole slaw, dill pickles and pickled beets. Or choose from a variety of hearty dishes that may include chicken in the pot or potato pancakes and apple sauce.

Cream cheese and lox (smoked salmon) on a bagel (a kind of hard roll) ranks high among kosher specialities, along with chopped liver and pastrami (highly seasoned smoked beef).

Coffee shops and self-service cafeterias offer hamburgers, French fries (chips), home-style cooking and pastries. They do not serve alcoholic drinks.

Fast food chains. McDonald's, Kentucky Fried Chicken and Burger King are just a few of the short-order establishments that line Florida's streets and highways. Prices are very cheap, but you have to eat at picnic tables, or perhaps standing up, if you don't take the food away with you.

"Ethnic" restaurants of every sort figure on the Florida gastronomy scene: Greek, Mexican, Chinese, Spanish, Italian and French—even British pubs and restaurants serving fish and chips.

Cuban restaurants and coffee bars serve traditional Creole dishes and little cups of steaming *café cubano*. The better part of Cuban eating houses are to be found in Miami's Little Havana and Tampa's Ybor City, although these areas have no monopoly on Creole cuisine.

A perennial favourite is the Cuban sandwich—slices of pork, ham and cheese combined with lettuce, mayonnaise and pickles on crusty Cuban bread. And then there is the *perro caliente*—nothing more or less than a good old American hot dog.

Health restaurants and juice bars. Some are strictly vegetarian, while others offer fresh fish; in general, the standard of cooking and quality is high. The emphasis is on organically grown produce—the bounty

of the Sunshine State. Fruit salads will never be fresher, nor vegetables more imaginatively prepared.

What to Eat
Breakfast Specialities. Start the day with Continental breakfast: orange or grapefruit juice, coffee and toast (whole wheat, rye and pumpernickel are often available) or Danish pastry (a sweet roll). Or choose eggs, grits, sausages, pancakes, French toast or waffles. Bagels often appear on the breakfast table. Pancake houses and coffee shops serve breakfast specialities all day long.

English visitors may find American coffee rather weak; however, it is customary to drink several cups and refills are offered as a matter of course.

Soups. You can almost make a meal of thick and filling mushroom-barley or navy bean soup. Don't overlook Cuban black bean soup. Conch chowder, available on the Keys, combines milk, potatoes, vegetables and chopped conch, a type of shellfish. Turtle soup is another Keys speciality.

Salads. Many restaurants allow customers to serve themselves from the salad bar; lettuce, raw vegetables, bean sprouts, soya beans, cottage cheese and chopped bacon make a colourful display. Otherwise, a salad usually consists of lettuce, tomatoes and cucumber. Dressings include French (the creamy recipe varies from chef to chef), Italian (oil, vinegar, garlic), Blue Cheese or Roquefort, Thousand Island (mayonnaise, pickle, tomato ketchup, hard-boiled egg) and Russian (mayonnaise and chili sauce).

Salads are popular for lunch: chef's salad, made with ham, cheese, chicken or other cold meats and lettuce; Caesar salad, or romaine lettuce, anchovies and croutons tossed with a tangy cheese and garlic dressing; and raw spinach salad. Fruit salad may comprise juicy oranges, papaya, mango, starfruit, grapefruit, cantaloupe, watermelon or pineapple, depending on the season. Frozen yoghurt, cottage cheese or small sandwiches of date-nut bread are the usual accompaniments.

Seafood. Warm Florida waters teem with fish and shellfish: red snapper, yellowtail, grouper, jumbo shrimp, stone crab and crawfish ("Florida lobster"). Don't be afraid to order dolphin, a tasty fish that bears no relation to Flipper. Nothing compares with the flavour of freshly caught broiled fish, served with a simple lemon and butter sauce. Shrimp are best broiled, fried, or steamed in beer. Or, of course, cold, as a jumbo shrimp cocktail served with a chili sauce spiked with horseradish.

Stone crabs, a seasonal delicacy, have a devoted following all over southern Florida. Diners often don bibs to eat the meat, which is extracted from the claws with the aid of a nutcracker and dipped into a sauce of lemon-butter or mustard-mayonnaise.

If the vast array of Florida seafood confuses you, order a combination seafood platter, a sampling of the catch of the day, served hot or cold. Meat lovers can satisfy their passion for steak and eat seafood, too. Ask for "surf and turf", a steak and seafood platter.

Hamburgers are pure Americana: fast, cheap and full of flavour.

You'll probably acquire a taste for turtle steak or conch fritters if you eat them on the Keys. Chefs inland favour catfish, a freshwater variety that is fried and served with hush puppies.

Meat. Steaks, roast beef and southern fried chicken take pride of place. French fries (chips) or a baked potato are the inevitable accompaniments. Order your steak rare (underdone), medium or well done.

Ham steak, a southern speciality, is often garnished with pineapple; stuffed turkey graces menus year-round. Fried Florida frogs' legs are a regional speciality, and spare ribs can be eaten all over the state.

Most Cuban restaurants offer *picadillo* (marinated ground beef mixed with olives, green peppers, garlic, onions and tomato sauce) and *arroz con pollo* (chicken and rice). A popular Mexican-American dish is *enchilada*, a tortilla (cornmeal pancake) stuffed with a meat filling and baked with sauce. *Tacos*, deep-fried tortillas, and *tostadas*, crisp tortilla strips, can be eaten with

Cocktails for two in a quiet lounge end an afternoon nicely.

guacamole, an avocado paste.

Vegetables. Apart from health food and some ethnic restaurants, cooked vegetables are not served in great variety; salads generally take their place. A notable exception is fresh corn on the cob (ears of sweet corn). Southern-style gumbos represent the best of home cooking. Yams, candied and baked, are another legacy of the Old South.

Cheese. Americans rarely eat cheese after a meal, but rather as fillings in generous sandwiches. Choose "Swiss", "Dutch", American or American Cheddar. Cream cheese will never taste better than it does on a bagel. Cottage cheese often garnishes fruit and vegetable salads.

Desserts. You'll be tempted by dozens of different kinds of sundaes and parfaits (alternate layers of fruit or sauce and ice cream in a tall dessert glass). Frozen yoghurt in fruit flavours is popular too.

Order sweet and creamy Key lime pie anywhere in Florida, but especially on the Keys. You'll also enjoy Boston cream pie, a sponge cake filled with custard and topped with rich chocolate. Cheese cake reigns supreme in half a dozen varieties (strawberry, blueberry, pineapple...).

Drinks

Soft drinks, especially the cola type, lead in popularity. You can always ask for an artificially sweetened one. Iced water and iced tea are served with meals year-round.

Ice cold beer is comparable to British lager. You can also find pale or brown ale and many foreign beers either imported or manufactured under licence.

Order domestic wine by the bottle, carafe, or generous glass. Both French and Italian wines are quite expensive, and generally no better than a good California brand. Bear in mind that many restaurants, especially the ethnic ones, have no liquor licence; it is perfectly acceptable to bring your own bottle of wine to these establishments.

Cocktails, blended from rum, tequila, and tropical fruit juices, are served by the glass or, more economically, by the pitcher. The ever-popular *piña colada* combines rum, pineapple juice and coconut milk. Daiquiris are made with rum and an assortment of fruit juices—peach, strawberry or banana, for example. Orange juice and grenadine are combined in the potent Tequila Sunrise, and a Margarita has fresh lime, tequila and ice.

Parking, Prices and Tipping

Some restaurants provide valet parking for your car—a great convenience where parking spaces are few and far between. Drive up to the entrance and leave you car with an attendant, who will give you a numbered ticket. You usually have to pay a small fee.

Many restaurants charge more for dinner than for lunch. In simple eating houses, you often pay the cashier on your way out, after leaving a tip on the table.

Florida Gold

Americans who can't get away for a sunny Florida holiday may still have some Florida sunshine sent to them—in the form of golden citrus fruit. The state's vast citrus groves produce millions of bushels of fruit every year. Groves both large and small have assortments all packed in sturdy boxes to be mailed off as soon as an order is received.

The variety of Florida citrus produce already seems endless, and yet new types continue to be developed every year. Here are some of the most popular ones:

Navel oranges: Large, thin-skinned and juicy, navels peel easily and are a favourite at snack-time. Season: November–January.

Temple oranges: Richer in flavour than navels, Temples are easy to peel—much like a tangerine—and virtually seedless. Temples ripen in January and February only.

Valencia oranges: The late-ripeners, Valencias come to the fruit stands in March and are available till May. They're particularly tasty in fruit salads.

Tangerines: Quickest juicy snack of all, Robinson tangerines ripen in October and November; in December and January, you'll find the Dancy variety; in March, look for the extra-sweet and delicious Honey tangerines.

Tangelos: A Florida hybrid, tangelos combine the easy-eating qualities of the tangerine with the zesty flavour of a sweet grapefruit. Orlando tangerines ripen in November and December, red "Minneolas" in January.

Grapefruit: From the Indian River district, the Marsh Whites have a nobler, austere sourness while the Ruby Reds are sweeter.

Kumquats: Farmers often give away these delicious little treats, which look like miniature, oval oranges. Pop the whole thing in your mouth, and chew the sweet rind along with the zest. Ask for some when you buy fruit.

How to Get There

Although the fares and conditions described below have all been carefully checked, it is advisable to consult a travel agent for the latest information on fares and other arrangements.

From North America

BY AIR: Miami, Ft. Lauderdale, Orlando (the airport closest to Disney World), Tampa, St. Petersburg and Sarasota are easily accessible from the larger northern, midwestern and western cities. There are several non-stop flights every day to Miami from New York, Chicago, Los Angeles and San Francisco. Direct flights link Chicago, New York and Los Angeles with Tampa every day. Coming from Chicago or New York, you can choose from over a dozen daily, direct flights to Orlando, or several one-stop flights from Los Angeles and San Francisco.

BY BUS: Florida destinations are served by Trailways and Greyhound coach.

BY RAIL: Amtrak is currently advertising a variety of bargain fares, including Excursion and Family fares and tour packages with hotel and guide included.

BY CAR: Travellers coming down the east coast can take Interstate 95 via Washington and Savannah. The toll turnpike system, another possibility, links up with the Sunshine State Parkway. The shortest route from the west coast is Interstate 10, passing Tucson, El Paso, Houston and Mobile.

From Great Britain

BY AIR: There are daily non-stop flights from Heathrow to Miami and Tampa, and connecting flights to Orlando. Fares available include first class, two grades of economy, Excursion, APEX (Advance Purchase Excursion), Super-APEX, and Standby. The Excursion fare, valid for a period of 14 to 60 days, requires no advance booking. APEX and Super-APEX must be booked 21 days in advance for stays of 7 to 180 days. Children fly for two-thirds of the APEX fare.

Some U.S. airlines offer travellers from abroad a discount on the cost of each internal flight, or flat-rate unlimited-travel tickets for specific periods.

Charter Flights and Package Tours: Advance Booking Charter (ABC) flights from London to Miami must be booked three weeks in advance. Many package tours are available: camper holidays, coach tours, excursions to Disney World or the Bahamas, trips to other American cities and sights, etc. Many Caribbean cruises originate in Miami, "cruise capital of the world".

Baggage. Baggage allowances for scheduled transatlantic flights are complex, but you are allowed to check in, free, two suitcases of normal size. In addition, one piece of hand baggage of a size which fits easily under the aircraft seat may be carried on board. Confirm size and weight restrictions with your travel agent or air carrier when booking your ticket.

It is advisable to insure all luggage for the duration of your trip. Any travel agent can make the necessary arrangements.

When to Go

Most of the year, Florida weather ranges from warm to hot, but the coasts are agreeably cooled by ocean breezes. Inland temperatures are usually higher. The peak tourist season is winter, when temperatures and precipitation are at their lowest. You may encounter a brief spell of cool weather, but the thermometer rarely drops low enough to interfere with swimming and sunbathing. If you can, visit Florida during the pleasant off-season months, April–May or October–November.

Average maximum daytime and sea temperatures for Miami:

		J	F	M	A	M	J	J	A	S	O	N	D
Air	°C	23	24	25	26	28	30	31	31	30	28	26	24
	°F	74	75	77	78	82	86	88	88	86	82	78	75
Water	°C	22	23	24	25	28	30	31	32	30	28	25	23
	°F	72	74	75	77	82	86	88	90	86	82	77	74

Planning Your Budget

To give you an idea of what to expect, here's a list of average prices. However, they must be regarded as approximate and taken as broad guidelines; inflation continues to push prices upwards.

Airport transfer. Taxi from Miami International Airport to Miami Beach $20–25. Red Top Sedan Service $6–9, depending on destination. Taxi Orlando International Airport to Disney World $25, bus $6.50.

Baby-sitters. $3.50 per hour, 50¢ for each additional child, plus transport expenses.

Bicycle hire. $3 per hour, $15 per day, $35 per week (three-speed).

Campground. $6 and up per day, per site (space).

Car hire. Prices in Florida vary tremendously according to the company and the season. Investigate both national and local firms and compare prices with the following rate for a medium-priced car (Chevrolet Citation) with unlimited mileage: $34 per day, $120 per week.

Cigarettes (20). American $1.50, foreign brands higher.

Disney World. *One-day ticket* (Magic Kingdom or EPCOT Center) adult $21.50, child (3–12) $18.50. *Three-day World Passport* adult $53.50, child $45.50.

Entertainment. *Cinema* $3.50–7, *nightclub/discotheque* $5–10 for cover charge, $3–5 for drinks.

Hairdressers. *Man's* haircut $15–25. *Woman's* haircut $15–25, cut, shampoo and set $15–30, colour rinse/dye $10–15.

Hotels (double room with bath). *De luxe* $100 and up, *moderate* $60–80, *budget* $30–60.

Laundry. Shirt $1, blouse $3.75. **Dry-cleaning:** jacket $2.50–3.50, trousers $2.25–3.50, dress $5.50–7.

Meals and drinks. Continental breakfast $2–5, full breakfast $4–10, lunch in snack bar $5, in restaurant $7.50–15, dinner $15–30 (more with entertainment); coffee $1, espresso $1.50–2, beer $2–2.50, glass of wine $2–2.50, carafe $6–7, bottle $10 and up, cocktail $2–4.

Swamp airboat rides (45 minutes). $5–8.

Taxis. Meters start on $1, plus $1.20 per mile.

BLUEPRINT for a Perfect Trip

An A-Z Summary of Practical Information and Facts

Contents

ACCOMMODATION (see also CAMPING). The Florida Hotel and Motel Association publishes a free *Florida Hotel & Motel Travelers Guide.* Write to:

P.O. Box 1529, Tallahassee, FL 32302, or phone (904) 224-2888

Reservations for hotels in Greater Miami can be made 24 hours a day without charge by dialling the Greater Miami Reservation System, tel. (305) 532-9667 (collect, within Florida) or 800-821-2183 (toll-free, from outside the state).

Florida offers a huge variety of accommodation in every price range. But in high season reservations are hard to come by, especially at Disney World and in the popular beach resorts. Book well in advance: six months or a year may not be too much for the Christmas and Easter holidays. (Check-in time usually starts at 3 p.m., check-out time at 11 a.m. or 12 noon.) A resort tax of 5% (7% in Surfside and Bal Harbour) is added to hotel bills in Greater Miami. Florida State sales tax amounts to an additional 5%.

American hotels and motels usually charge by the room, not by the number of occupants. Most rooms have two double beds, private bathroom and a colour television. "Efficiencies" are rooms with kitchenette or separate kitchen and dining area. Facilities include dishes, pans and cutlery.

In coastal areas, the most expensive hotels are generally situated directly on the beach; the further from the beach you go, the lower the rates should be. Rooms facing a pool or garden are often two-thirds the price of rooms with an ocean view.

A group of renovated ocean-front hotels from the 1930s—Art Deco Hotels—attracts a trendy young crowd to the south shore of Miami Beach. Smaller and more personal than the newer beach resorts, these old hotels feature Jazz Age-era atmosphere in sight of the sea.

High season in Florida is from December 15 to March or April. The quietest times are May to June and September to November, when prices are lower.

A

A   Some resort hotels offer special rates to guests who take their meals on the premises: A.P. (American Plan) includes three meals a day and M.A.P. (Modified American Plan), breakfast and lunch or dinner.

Larger hotels and motels employ a hotel porter (bell captain) who can arrange tours, call for a cab or hire a car for you. Visitors on a budget can economize by making their own arrangements.

Youth hostels. Unlike Europe, the U.S. is not well endowed with youth hostels. There are, nevertheless, 160-odd hostels scattered throughout the country. Most are situated outside the big cities, and the distances between them can be enormous, so you cannot simply (as in Europe) travel from hostel to hostel. There is no age limit. For further information, apply to:

American Youth Hostel Association, Inc., National Campus, Delaplane, VA 22025

AIRPORTS. Miami International Airport is a huge, crowded and confusing place, just west of the city centre. It's served by more than 50 airlines, and is one of the world's busiest. The airport has two terminals, the main building and a satellite terminal for many international flights. They are connected by an automated "peoplemover".

The new customs and immigration building, located behind the main terminal, is linked to the satellite terminal by two shuttle trains. Red and green channels are in operation and generally speaking customs formalities are simple and quick.

The satellite terminal has a transit lounge (8 hours maximum stay) for passengers continuing to an international destination, and there are shops, a snack restaurant, telephones and a duty-free shop.

The main terminal, divided into concourses (or zones) consists of two floors, the lower level domestic-arrival area and the upper level departure and ticket concourse. Here you'll find bars, snack-bars, fast-food restaurants, telephones, shops and an information desk open 24 hours a day. If you're not well supplied with dollars, change money at one of the airport's currency-exchange counters. It's unwise to go into town without sufficient U.S. currency (and a major credit card). Baggage claim (show your ticket-stubs to security guards) and car hire is downstairs. The airport has its own hotel. Enter at Zone E in the main terminal building.

Ground transport*. From Miami International, a taxi to Miami Beach usually takes 15–25 minutes (up to an hour in rush periods). The bright blue vehicles of the Airport Region Taxi Service (ARTS) carry passengers to nearby destinations for a low, flat fare. Minibuses ("Red-Top") lined up at the kerb will take you to almost any hotel downtown or on Miami Beach for a third of the price of a regular taxi. Cheaper still are the municipal buses, leaving every 30–45 minutes from a stop outside the main terminal's lower level.

Check-in time. Arrive 45 minutes before domestic flights, one hour before international. For flight information, call your airline.

Other Florida airports. Some of Florida's main tourist attractions are situated near airports. Disney World, for example, can be reached via Orlando International Airport. Key West has its own international airport. The main airports on the west coast are at Tampa and Fort Myers; in the north, at Jacksonville, Tallahassee and Pensacola.

Car hire agencies are represented at all of Florida's bigger airports, and it's often possible to rent a car at one airport and return it at another. Many agencies provide free transport from airports to their offices.

Domestic flights. Air travel is by far the quickest and most convenient way of getting round the U.S., though prices are higher since deregulation. The most-travelled routes have shuttle-services, where the plane simply takes off when full. Travellers from abroad have a chance on most airlines of getting a *Visit U.S.A.* ticket, which provides substantial discounts and sets no fixed programme. To benefit from these reduced-price tickets, you must buy them before you arrive in the U.S.A. (or within 15 days of arrival).

Fares change constantly, so it would be wise to consult a travel agent for the latest information about discounts and special deals.

BABY-SITTERS*. The best hotels employ a full-time baby-sitter. Other hotels and motels provide lists of reliable sitters or names of agencies on call. Failing that, the yellow pages of the telephone directory list sitters and agencies licensed by the State of Florida under the heading "Sitting Services". There is a four-hour minimum charge, plus travel expenses.

CAMPING*. Camping in America generally involves recreational vehicles—campers, motor homes or caravans (trailers). So that if you are camping the American way, follow the indispensable *Rand McNally Campground and Trailer Park Guide* or the voluminous

A

B

C

109

C *Woodalls.* Both list campsites, grading them according to their facilities. You shouldn't be without the *Florida State Parks Guide*, a map of all the excellent state parks (about 40) and state recreational areas with camping facilities, available from:

Florida Department of Natural Resources
Bureau of Education and Information
3900 Commonwealth Boulevard
Tallahassee, FL 32303

In each state park, length of stay is limited to two weeks. To avoid disappointment, it's essential to reserve a place in advance by telephone.

Camping beside the road—or on private land without permission—is both illegal and unsafe.

CAR HIRE* and DRIVING. Stiff competition among Florida's car hire companies ensures that rates within the state are relatively low. If you can pick up and return the car at the same place, try one of the local businesses. If, on the other hand, you will be dropping it off in another city, go to one of the international companies.

The well-known car hire agencies charge higher rental rates, but often include insurance costs in the price; the small companies, however, having little or no insurance included in the rates, offer an option (take it!) to buy fairly inexpensive insurance coverage per day or per week.

Drivers over 21 with a valid driving licence can hire a car. Some agencies make exceptions for 18-year-old drivers paying with a credit card. For tourists from non-English-speaking countries, a translation of the driving licence is highly recommended, together with the national licence itself, or failing this, an International Driving Permit.

Invariably, it is more convenient to make payment with a major credit card rather than cash. If you have no card, you must pay a deposit. Sometimes cash is refused at night and on weekends.

To extend your hire, inform the original office, or stop at the nearest branch office if you have to pay another deposit.

On the road. Drive on the right. In Florida, you are allowed to turn right after a stop at a red light, provided that there is no cross-traffic, that you have given way to pedestrians and that there is no sign to the contrary. When you park, your car must point in the same direction as the flow of traffic. Never drive at night without headlights, it's strictly illegal. Lane discipline is more rigorous than in Europe, so don't weave. For additional information on Florida road rules, see the book *Florida Driver's Handbook* published by the Highway Patrol.

Highways (motorways). There are several different types of roads in Florida, and many collect tolls. Toll highways are called turnpikes, and high-speed divided highways are called expressways. You should keep a stock of change for convenience when travelling; most toll areas provide a basket into which you drop the right change, so there's no waiting.

Expressway driving follows certain rules of the road. Rather than accelerate up the ramp (slip road) to join the traffic at its own speed, you hesitate at the top of the ramp and wait for an opening. A national speed limit of 55 mph operates on highways, though in actual fact, expressway traffic may move at a slightly faster pace. If you keep up with the flow of traffic, you'll have no problem, but go any faster, and a patrol car will pull you over. You can, at least, take comfort in the knowledge that American police are generally kind to foreigners.

If you have a breakdown on an expressway, pull over onto the right-hand shoulder, tie a handkerchief to the doorhandle or radio aerial, raise the bonnet (hood) and wait in the car for assistance. At night, use the blinker.

Petrol (gas) and services. Florida's service stations have both self-service and full-service pumps. In some areas it is necessary to have the exact amount of purchase at night. Note that many petrol stations close in the evenings and on weekends, particularly on Sundays.

Most rental-cars in Florida are equipped with air-conditioners; if your car is running out of petrol or overheating, turn off the cooling system—it's a strain on the engine.

Parking. Florida's famous attractions usually have large and inexpensive (often free) car parks. Most municipal car parks have meters; coins required and length of stay authorized, etc., are always noted on them. Parallel and angle parking spaces in the streets are indicated by white lines painted on the asphalt. Do not park by a fire hydrant or alongside a kerb painted yellow.

American Automobile Association. The AAA offers assistance to members of affiliated organizations abroad. It also provides travel information for the U.S. and can arrange automobile insurance by the month for owner-drivers. Contact AAA World Travel:

8111 Gatehouse Road, Falls Church, VA 22047.

C **Road signs.** Although the U.S. has begun to change over to international road signs, progress has been gradual, and some differences remain between international and U.S. signs. The following list shows some of the different British and U.S. terms.

American	British
Detour	Deviation
Divided highway	Dual carriageway
Expressway	Motorway
Men working	Roadworks
No passing	No overtaking
No parking along highway	Clearway
Railroad crossing	Level crossing
Roadway	Carriageway
Traffic circle	Roundabout
Yield	Give way

CIGARETTES, CIGARS, TOBACCO*. Packets of cigarettes may vary in price by as much as one third more or less, depending on where you buy them. A packet from a vending machine always costs much more than one obtained in a supermarket or at a news-stand. Naturally, cigarettes are cheaper when bought by the carton.

The choice of pipe tobacco, both home-grown and imported, is vast, and Cuban artisans still roll cigars by hand in Tampa and Miami.

CLIMATE and CLOTHING (see also WHEN TO GO, p. 104). Some tourist brochures boast that you'll never need warm clothing, even in the middle of winter, but prudence suggests otherwise. In winter, Atlantic coast beaches can be very windy, while the northern and central areas have some rainy days and cold spells. Even in the south, temperatures *can* dip to near freezing for short periods. On the other hand, there are many winter days when temperatures reach the 80's, especially in south Florida and on the Keys, so be sure to pack clothing for every eventuality.

During the sweltering days of summer, Floridians turn on their air-conditioners. Bear in mind that these highly efficient machines can blow with an arctic vengeance, so don't forget to take a wrap with you when shopping, dining out or riding in air-conditioned vehicles—including the city buses.

In resort towns, casual city attire is appropriate round the clock. If
112 you're likely to go swimming often, bring a spare bathing costume for

a rapid change. Other useful items to tuck into your suitcase include binoculars for viewing bird life, especially in the Everglades, and sturdy shoes for hiking along rocky trails.

For a weather report, dial 661-5065 in Miami.

COMMUNICATIONS

Post offices. The U.S. postal service deals only with mail. Telephone and telegraph services are operated by other companies. Post your letters in the blue kerbside boxes. You can purchase stamps from machines in post office entrance halls after hours. Hotel receptionists usually sell stamps.

Post office hours are from 8 a.m. to 5 p.m., Monday to Friday, from 8 a.m. to 12 noon on Saturdays. In larger towns, one branch usually remains open later in the evening, till 9 p.m. or so.

Poste restante (general delivery). You can have mail marked "General Delivery" sent to you care of the main post office of any town. The letters will be held for no more than a month. American Express offices also keep post for 30 days; envelopes should be marked "Client's Mail".

Take your driving licence or passport with you for identification.

Telegrams. American telegraph companies are privately run. They offer domestic and overseas services, as well as domestic telex facilities, and are listed in the yellow pages. You can telephone the telegraph office, dictate the message and have the charge added to your hotel bill, or dictate it from a coin-operated phone and pay on the spot. A letter telegram (night letter) costs about half the rate of a normal telegram.

Telephone. The independent American telephone systems are efficient and reliable. Phone boxes are found in the streets, at many service stations, in shopping plazas, in restaurants and in most public buildings. Directions for use are posted on the instrument.

To make a local call, lift the receiver, deposit 25¢ in the proper slot, wait for the dialling tone, then dial (or push-button dial) the seven-digit number. If your call is more than 25¢, the operator will automatically inform you of any additional charge, so have some change ready. For local information, ring 411.

Long-distance and many international calls may be dialled direct, even from a pay phone if you follow the posted directions. If you don't

C know the correct area code, dial "O" for operator assistance. Long-distance calls cost more from a pay phone than from a private one.

Telephone rates are listed in the introduction to the white pages of the telephone directory. Also included is information on personal (person-to-person), reverse-charge (collect) and credit card calls. All numbers with an 800 prefix are toll-free. Cheapest calls are from a private phone at night, weekends and holidays.

COMPLAINTS. If you have a serious complaint about certain business practices and have talked with the manager of the establishment in question to no avail, you may contact the Agriculture Department: Consumer Services Division, The Capitol, Tallahassee, FL 32301; tel. 1-800-342-2176

CONSULATES. No English-speaking country (not even Canada) has a consulate in Florida.

Australia:	636 5th Avenue, New York; tel. (212) 245-4000
Canada:	1251 Avenue of the Americas, New York; tel. (212) 586-2400
Eire:	515 Madison Avenue, New York; tel. (212) 319-2555
New Zealand:	Suite 530, 630 5th Avenue, New York; tel. (212) 586-0060
South Africa:	425 Park Avenue, New York; tel. (212) 838-1700
United Kingdom:	225 Peachtree Street N.E., Atlanta, Georgia; tel. (404) 524-5856

CUSTOMS and ENTRY REGULATIONS. Canadians need only evidence of their nationality to enter the U.S. Other foreign visitors require a visa, obtainable at U.S. embassies and consulates abroad. The application process *can* prove slow and difficult depending on individual circumstances. When you apply, take documents along which will verify that you intend to return home.

Duty-free allowance. You will be asked to fill out a customs declaration form before you arrive in the U.S. The following chart shows what main duty-free items you may take into the U.S. (if you are over **114** 21) and, when returning home, into your own country:

Into:	Cigarettes	Cigars	Tobacco	Spirits	Wine
U.S.A.	200	or 50	or 1,350 g.	1 l.	or 1 l.
Australia	200	or 250 g. or	250 g.	1 l.	or 1 l.
Canada	200	and 50 and	900 g.	1.1 l.	or 1.1 l.
Eire	200	or 50	or 250 g.	1 l.	and 2 l.
N. Zealand	200	or 50	or 250 g.	1.1 l.	and 4.5 l.
S. Africa	400	and 50 and	250 g.	1 l.	and 2 l.
U.K.	200	or 50	or 250 g.	1 l.	and 2 l.

A non-resident may claim, free of duty and taxes, articles up to $100 in value for use as gifts for other persons. The exemption is valid only if the gifts accompany you, if you stay 72 hours or more and have not claimed this exemption within the preceding 6 months. 100 cigars may be included within this gift exemption.

Plants and foodstuffs also are subject to strict control; visitors from abroad may not import fruits, vegetables or meat. The same goes for chocolates that contain liqueur.

Arriving and departing passengers should report any money or cheques, etc. exceeding a total of $10,000.

DRUGS. Buying and selling hard drugs is a serious offence. Florida has a large force of undercover officers (plain-clothes policemen), who are battling to keep drugs out of the U.S.

D

ELECTRIC CURRENT. The U.S. has 110–115-volt 60-cycle A.C. Plugs are small, flat and two-pronged; foreigners will need an adaptor for shavers, etc.

E

EMERGENCIES. Dial 911, and the operator will ask if you want police, ambulance or the fire department.

All towns and cities have a 24-hour number to call for emergency, if you need a doctor or a dentist. For a dentist in the Miami area phone 667-3647. For a doctor, the number is 326-1177.

G **GUIDES and TOURS.** Some of the larger attractions provide the services of a guide. At the Magic Kingdom, Disney World, ask for a guide at the Town Hall; in Epcot Center inquire at Earth Station. A group of foreign-language guides are on call to take visitors on a quick tour, including a selection of rides.

Sightseeing tours by bus are available in cities such as Miami, Orlando, Tampa and St. Petersburg. Attractions like Disney World, Kennedy Space Center, Busch Gardens, St. Augustine and many more can be visited on guided tours. There are one-day bus tours from Miami to Disney World, but these are not recommended. Instead, look into day trips organized by the airlines. Check with a travel agent for details.

You can take pleasure cruises from many resorts, touring the coast, the inlets, lakes, rivers and swamps, often stopping at a restaurant for lunch. Miami and Miami Beach are particularly well served, with tours and cruises of varying lengths up and down the coast, including one to the Seaquarium. At Marathon, you can take a glass-bottomed boat out to view the coral reefs, and a diver goes down to feed fish. In other towns, tours and cruises are also available, notably in St. Petersburg, Sarasota, Naples, Tarpon Springs and Key West.

H **HEALTH and MEDICAL CARE** (see also EMERGENCIES). Foreigners should note the U.S. doesn't provide free medical services, and that medical treatment is expensive. Arrangements should therefore be made in advance for temporary health insurance (through a travel agent or an insurance company); alternatively, ask at the local Social Security office for precise information on coverage during your trip.

Emergency rooms of hospitals will treat anyone in need of speedy attention, including hospitalization in a community ward.

If you arrive in Florida after flying through several time zones, take it easy the first couple of days. Doctors recommend visitors to eat lightly initially, and to get plenty of rest.

Beware of the powerful sun. Start with a sun-cream screen or complete-block cream at first and build up a tan gradually in small doses.

Visitors from Great Britain will find that a certain number of drugs sold over the counter at home can only be purchased by prescription in the U.S. There's no shortage of drugstores, or pharmacies, a few of them open late at night.

HIKING and CANOEING. The Florida Trail is a 1,300-mile footpath running the length of the state. Anyone may hike along it through national forests and state parks; only members of the Florida Trail

Association, however, are allowed across parts on private property. It isn't expensive to take out a year's membership; alternatively, non-residents may apply for a permit good for 60 days' use of the trail. The association offers organized tours through sections of the trail, including a number of one-day and overnight canoe trips. For further details, write to:

Florida Trail Association Inc., P.O. Box 13708, Gainesville, FL 32604

There are some 35 official canoe trails in Florida, established by the Florida Department of Natural Resources (for address, see under CAMPING). Canoes can be hired through rental agencies listed in the yellow pages of the telephone directory under "Boat Dealers", or ask at the local chamber of commerce. The free *Guide to Florida Canoe Trails* shows the recommended starting and finishing points of the official canoe routes and gives tips about individual trails.

HITCH-HIKING. The FBI and police advise strongly against hitch-hiking, and it is illegal on highways (motorways) and along the Florida Keys.

HOURS (see also COMMUNICATIONS and MONEY MATTERS). Most shops and tourist businesses are open from 8 or 9 a.m. (larger stores from 9.30 or 10 a.m.) to 5 or 6 p.m. Some stores and chain-restaurants never close. Small restaurants usually open at 6 a.m. and close by 11 p.m.

Below are listed the opening hours of most of the sites mentioned in our guide. As a general rule, however, it's always worth telephoning ahead of time to check. In many cases, hours are extended considerably during holiday periods.

Walt Disney World. Most attractions are open daily from 9 a.m. to 9 p.m. At peak times (Christmas and Easter weeks, national holidays, summer), the gates open at 8 a.m. or earlier and close as late as midnight.

Kennedy Space Center. Daily except Christmas Day from 8 a.m. until two hours before sunset.

Marineland of Florida. 8 a.m.–6 p.m. daily.

Miami

Fairchild Tropical Garden. 9.30 a.m.–4.30 p.m. daily.

Historical Museum of Southern Florida. 9 a.m.–5 p.m., Monday–Saturday, Sunday 12.30–5 p.m.

Lowe Art Museum. 10 a.m.–5 p.m., Tuesday–Saturday, 2–5 p.m. Sunday.

Metrozoo. 10 a.m.–5.30 p.m. daily (box office closes at 4 p.m.).

Monkey Jungle. 9.30 a.m.–5 p.m. daily.

Museum of Science, 9 a.m.–10 p.m., Monday–Saturday, Sunday 12.30–10 p.m.

Orchid Jungle. 8.30 a.m.–5.30 p.m. daily.

Parrot Jungle. 9.30 a.m.–5 p.m. daily.

Planet Ocean. 10 a.m.–6 p.m. daily (box office closes at 4.30 p.m.).

St. Bernard's Monastery. 10 a.m.–5 p.m. Monday–Saturday, Sunday 12 noon–5 p.m.

Miami Seaquarium. 9 a.m.–6.30 p.m. (box office closes at 5 p.m.).

Vizcaya. 9.30 a.m.–5 p.m. daily except Christmas Day (Saturday and Sunday also 7.30–9.30 p.m.).

Fort Lauderdale

Ocean World. From 10 a.m. daily (box office closes at 4.15 p.m.).

Fort Myers

Edison Winter Home. 9 a.m.–4 p.m., Monday–Saturday, Sunday 12.30 a.m.–4.30 p.m.

Key West

Audubon House. 9 a.m.–12 noon and 1–5 p.m. daily.

Ernest Hemingway House. 9 a.m.–5 p.m. daily.

Orlando

Circus World. 9 a.m.–6 p.m. daily.

Sea World. 9 a.m.–7 p.m. in winter, 8.30 a.m.–8 p.m. in summer.

Palm Beach

Henry Morrison Flagler Museum. 10 a.m.–5 p.m., Tuesday to Sunday.

Lion Country Safari. 9.30 a.m.–4.30 p.m. daily.

Norton Gallery of Art. 1–5 p.m. Saturday and Sunday only.

St. Augustine

Castillo de San Marcos. 8.30 a.m.–5.30 p.m. daily except Christmas Day.

Sarasota

Bellm's Cars and Music of Yesterday. 8.30 a.m.–6 p.m., Monday–Saturday, Sunday 9.30 a.m.–6 p.m.

Ringling Museums. 9 a.m.–10 p.m., Monday–Friday, 9 a.m.–5 p.m. on Saturday, 11 a.m.–6 p.m. on Sundays.

Tampa

Busch Gardens. 9.30 a.m.–6 p.m. in winter, till 8 p.m. in summer.

Winter Haven

Museum of Old Dolls and Toys. 10 a.m.–6 p.m., Monday–Saturday, Sunday 12 noon–5 p.m.

LANGUAGE. Miami is virtually a bi-lingual city, and such has been the influence of refugees, mainly from Cuba, that you'll hear lilting Spanish almost as much as English. Many welcome this Latin touch if others complain about the change in atmosphere. Miami's big enough to absorb it all.

Most English-speaking foreigners are now familiar with American words and phrases. However, here are a few which can be the source of confusion:

U.S.	British	U.S.	British
admission	entry fee	**minister**	vicar
bathroom	toilet (private)	**pavement**	road surface
bill	note (money)	**purse/pocketbook**	handbag
billfold	wallet	**rest room**	toilet (public)
check	bill (restaurant)	**round-trip**	return
collect call	reverse charges	(ticket)	
elevator	lift	**second floor**	first floor
first floor	ground floor	**sidewalk**	pavement
gasoline	petrol	**stand in line**	queue up
liquor	spirits	**trailer**	caravan
liquor store	off-licence	**underpass**	subway

LIQUOR REGULATIONS. You can buy beer and wine in many grocery stores, but spirits are sold in licensed liquor stores (off-licence) only. There are several strictly enforced laws. Tins of beer and wine or liquor bottles must not be displayed in public places—but be kept in bags at all times. In many counties within the state, it is prohibited to take alcoholic beverages onto the beaches.

L   You must be over 18 to purchase beer or any other alcoholic drink, or to buy any alcohol at a liquor store. You will be asked for identification (called "I.D.") of your age.

LOST PROPERTY. Air, rail and bus terminals and many stores have special "lost-and-found" areas. Restaurants put aside lost articles in the hope that someone will claim them. If your lost property is valuable, contact the police. If you lose your passport, get in touch with your consulate immediately.

M   **MAPS.** Florida welcome stations on main highways and ports of entry hand out free maps, and the local chamber of commerce or tourist authority will give you maps of the resort with attractions marked on them. Service stations dispense maps from vending machines, which are also found in hotel lobbies, at car hire agencies and in some grocery stores. All bookshops sell maps.

MEETING PEOPLE. The friendliest Floridians are found on the Keys; less so where tourists are more numerous, such as Miami Beach and along the Gold Coast. To meet other visitors easily and informally, there's no place like the hotel pool. Discos are a natural meeting-ground for young people.

   Britons enjoy a special place in American affections. Don't spoil the favourable prejudice by expecting things to be done exactly as at home; just relax and enjoy this dynamic and essentially friendly country.

MONEY MATTERS

Currency. The dollar is divided into 100 cents.

   Banknotes: $1, $2 (rare), $5, $10, $20, $50 and $100. Larger denominations are not in general circulation. All notes are the same shape and colour, so it is imperative to keep big and small notes in separate compartments of a wallet (i.e., never have $100 notes among a stack of $1s).

   Coins: 1¢ (called a "penny"), 5¢ ("nickel"), 10¢ ("dime"), 25¢ ("quarter"), 50¢ ("half dollar") and $1. You may inadvertently be given Canadian or other foreign coins in change. Canadian coins are worth about 10% less than U.S. ones, and they do not work in automatic machines, such as telephones.

Banks and currency exchange. Banking hours are usually from 9 a.m. to 4 p.m., Monday to Friday, but it's essential to note that very few banks change foreign currency. Disney World's banks are one notable exception. Even in major cities, there may be only one counter in one bank able to handle foreign money. American hotel receptionists are distrustful of foreign banknotes, and they may offer a low exchange rate (so be aware of the exact rate before changing money). It is simpler to travel with traveller's cheques (see below) denominated in dollars, major credit cards or cash in dollars.

When changing money or traveller's cheques, ask for $20 notes, which are accepted everywhere, as some establishments will refuse to accept larger notes unless they nearly equal the debt to be paid (e.g. a $100 note to pay a $95 hotel bill).

Credit cards. When buying merchandise, tickets, paying hotel or phone bills, you will be asked: "Cash or charge?", meaning you have the choice of paying either in cash or by credit card. Businesses are wary of little-known credit cards, but they'll gladly accept the top American or international cards, or those issued by major stores, gas (petrol) companies or top car hire agencies.

Many service stations and other businesses will not take money at night, only cards. Outside normal office hours, it's sometimes impossible to rent cars and pay bills with cash.

You'll need some form of identification when charging your purchase.

Traveller's cheques. Visitors from abroad may find traveller's cheques drawn on American banks easier to cash than those on foreign banks. Only cash small amounts at a time: keep the balance of your cheques in your hotel safe if possible. It's a good idea to follow instructions given for recording where and when you changed each cheque.

Prices. Most prices do not include a state sales tax of around 5%—and, in Greater Miami, a resort tax of 5% (7% in Surfside and Bal Harbour)—which is added to the hotel bill. The U.S. has a larger spread of prices for the same kind of item than you will find anywhere else, as well as a greater choice of objects. For moderately priced goods, visit the big department stores. Small independent grocery stores, drugstores and 24-hour "convenience stores" have price mark-ups of 10–70% over the supermarkets, but independent service stations are cheaper than those of the large oil companies.

NEWSPAPERS and MAGAZINES. Local newspapers and the national daily *USA Today* are sold in drugstores and from vending machines. Special news-stands carry the *New York Times* and the *Wall Street Journal,* as well as a variety of other newspapers. Three daily papers are printed in Miami: the *Miami Herald (El Miami*

N *Herald* in Spanish), the *Miami News* and the *Diario Las Américas.* The *Orlando Sentinel* provides information about central Florida. A local newspaper will put you in touch with community problems and give a timetable of TV programmes, opening hours of attractions, pages of grocery-store food bargains, and coupons for price reductions at various restaurants. Except for the local Spanish-language papers, you are unlikely to come across publications in another language unless you seek them out.

Most Floridian cities have their own magazine with articles on events.

P **PETS.** Few from outside the U.S. would think of bringing their pet on holiday; quarantine laws are so strict on return that it would hardly be worth it.

In many places, dogs are not allowed to run free, and they are usually barred from beaches, hotels, restaurants, foodshops and public transport. Disney World operates kennels for pets in several locations. A list of veterinarians can be found in the yellow pages.

PHOTOGRAPHY. Some of the larger attractions (Seaquarium, Disney World) loan or rent Polaroid cameras for use on their property.

Camera shops sell film, but drugstores and supermarkets supply the same—at discount prices. Wait until you are home to develop your film because it may take longer than you think. Film purchased in the U.S. can be developed in Britain and other European countries. Do not store film in the glove-compartment, or indeed anywhere in the car: in the sun, the car will get so hot that film will be ruined; the best place for it is in the refrigerator.

If your film goes through the airport security machine, it's quite likely to be ruined. Ask that it be checked separately, or buy a film-shield.

POLICE. City police are concerned with local crime and traffic violations, while Highway Patrol officers (also called State Troopers) ensure highway safety, and are on the lookout for people speeding or driving under the influence of alcohol or drugs.

The American police officer is surprisingly fair and friendly—often much more willing to believe extenuating circumstances than his British counterpart. After being baffled by your unfamiliar driving licence, he may address you familiarly by your first name and show some hesitation over giving you a ticket. Lucky you.

For emergencies, dial 911 (fire, police, ambulance).

PUBLIC HOLIDAYS. If a holiday, such as Christmas Day, falls on a Sunday, banks and most stores close on the following day. There are also long weekends (such as the one following Thanksgiving) when offices are closed for four days. Many restaurants never shut, however, not even at Christmas.

New Year's Day	January 1
Washington's Birthday *	Third Monday in February
Memorial Day	Last Monday in May
Independence Day	July 4
Labor Day	First Monday in September
Columbus Day *	Second Monday in October
Veterans' Day	November 11
Thanksgiving Day	Fourth Thursday in November
Christmas Day	December 25

* Shops and businesses open

RADIO and TV. There are numerous AM and FM radio stations, most broadcasting pop and country-and-western music, but each large city has at least one classical-music radio station.

Almost every hotel room has a television set. Programmes start at 6 a.m. and continue until about 3 in the morning. Florida news and sports programmes begin around 6 p.m., and national and international news programmes are beamed from New York at 6.30 or 7 p.m. Several networks run the news simultaneously.

Commercial American television aims to appeal to the largest possible number, and the amount of advertising tends to annoy those who are not familiar with it. The exception is the educational Public Broadcasting Service which screens music and drama programmes along with its own excellent news and information broadcasts. A variety of special-interest shows are aired on cable networks—but you have to pay for it.

RELIGIOUS SERVICES. Saturday newspapers often list the scheduled church services of the following day, with details of visiting preachers. Besides Catholic churches, there are American Presbyterian and Methodist churches and some branches of fundamentalist and southern Baptist denominations. In Miami Beach and along the Gold Coast there are numerous synagogues.

T **THEFT and CRIME.** Miami has theft problems similar to other big cities with transient populations, but elsewhere in Florida, there's little problem.

Most hotels have a safe for valuables. Never leave money, credit cards, cheque books, watches, cameras, etc., in a hotel room, but always in the safe.

In Miami, beware of pickpockets. They often work in pairs and frequent city buses, queues (lines), ticket counters, crowded stores and lifts (elevators).

Take the precaution of driving with windows up and doors locked in the centre of Miami, especially in crowded areas with numerous traffic lights. Thieves may attempt to open your car door or snatch your handbag through the window while you wait for the traffic light to change.

An unfortunate recent trend in the Miami area—not unique to the city but part of a worldwide phenomenon—is the increase in crimes of violence. To be on the safe side, go out after dark in groups, rather than alone, and avoid carrying large amounts of cash or valuables. It's a good idea to leave your car with the attendant at a restaurant, night club or discotheque, rather than parking it yourself on a dimly lit side street. If a tourist avoids certain areas, especially Liberty City in the north-west section of Miami, and follows the normal common sense rules of behaviour, he need not be apprehensive.

TIME and DATES. The continental U.S.A. has a total of four time zones; Florida (like New York City) is on Eastern Standard Time. In summer (between April and October) Daylight Saving Time is adopted and clocks move ahead one hour. The following chart shows the time in various cities in winter when it's noon in Florida:

Los Angeles	**Miami**	London	Sydney
9 a.m. Sunday	**noon Sunday**	5 p.m. Sunday	4 a.m. Monday

To get the exact time in Miami, call 324-8811.

Dates in the U.S.A. are written differently from those in Great Britain; for example, 1/6/99 means January 6, 1999.

TIPPING. Waiters and waitresses earn most of their salary from tips; often they are paid little else. Cinema or theatre ushers and filling-
station attendants are not tipped. Some further suggestions:

Guide	10–15%
Hairdresser / Barber	15%
Hotel maid, per day	$1
Lavatory attendant	50¢
Hotel porter, per bag	50¢–$1 (minimum $1)
Taxi driver	15%
Waiter	15%

TOILETS. You can find toilets in restaurants, railway stations and large stores. In some places you must deposit a dime, in others you should leave a tip for the attendant.

Americans use the terms "rest room", "powder room", "bathroom" (private) and "ladies" or "men's room" to indicate the toilet.

TOURIST INFORMATION AGENCIES. For information prior to arrival, write to:

United States Travel Service
22 Sackville Street
London W1 (tel. 01-439 7433)

or:

Florida Division of Tourism in Europe
55 Park Lane
London W1 (tel. 01-493 1343)

or:

State of Florida Division of Tourism
Department 468
Visitor Inquiry Section
126 Van Buren Street
Tallahassee, FL 32301 (tel. 904-487-1462)

There can be few places in the world with so much printed tourist literature. You are strongly advised to write ahead of time for brochures.

Information is freely dispensed from welcome stations on the main entry routes to the state and major points elsewhere, but the chief source of tourist information in any town or resort is the local chamber of commerce office.

T **TRANSPORT** (see also under AIRPORTS and CAR HIRE AND DRIVING)

Buses (see also GUIDES AND TOURS). The two largest coach companies, Greyhound Lines and Continental Trailways, offer state-wide service with stops at all major resorts and attractions (Miami–Key West in 5 hours). Quite apart from their state-wide network, they provide transport to and from cities all over the United States (New York to Orlando by express coach takes around 25 hours). Smaller bus lines provide a comprehensive local shuttle service between hotels and attractions, and also offer sightseeing tours. Beware of long-distance, one-day tours to major attractions; they don't always give sufficient time to visit.

Visitors can buy unlimited rover passes (these can only be bought outside the U.S.), good for a given length of time, to go anywhere in the country by bus at a flat rate.

City buses. Rule number one: always have the exact change ready to deposit in the box beside the driver. Miami buses can be crowded and frantic, but generally speaking, service is regular and punctual.

Miami Metrorail. Miami has the only rapid-transit system in the state of Florida, an elevated railway running from north to south through the centre of the city. Pay the exact fare in coins and proceed to the upper level platform. The air-conditioned trains operate at frequent intervals from 7 a.m. to midnight or 12.30 a.m.

Taxis*. Taxis may be painted one of several different colours, but they always carry a roof sign and can easily be recognized. Most taxis have meters, and the rates are generally painted on the doors. Some cruise the streets, especially in the city centres. To phone for a taxi, look in the yellow pages for your area under "Taxicabs". Tip 15% of the fare.

Trains. Amtrak (National Railroad Passenger Corporation) offers a variety of bargain fares, including Excursion and Family fares; the U.S.A. Railpass can only be purchased abroad, but many package tours are available in the U.S.

Good connections with comfortable, air-conditioned trains link Florida's main towns with centres throughout the U.S. (New York to Orlando takes 24 hours).

W **WEIGHTS and MEASURES.** The United States is one of the last countries in the world to change to the metric system, and is not yet involved in an official changeover programme.

Index

An asterisk (*) next to a page number indicates a map reference. For index to Practical Information, see page 106.